10 MINUTE
ZEN

FAIR WINDS
PRESS

10 MINUTE ZEN

Easy Tips to Lead You Down the Path of Enlightenment

COLLEEN SELL & ROSEMARY ROBERTS

First published in the U.S.A. by
Fair Winds Press
33 Commercial Street
Gloucester, Massachusetts 01930-5089

Library of Congress Cataloging-in-Publication Data available

ISBN 1-931412-23-5

Cover design by Laura Shaw Design
Book design by Leeann Leftwich Zajas
Printed and bound in Canada

10 9 8 7 6 5 4 3 2 1

For my father, Albert Lloyd Sell, whose loving-kindness
inspires loving-kindness.
— *Colleen Sell*

In dedication to my unwavering sister in spirit, Terri,
for her love and friendship as I learn to walk in my own light,
and to my son, Sean, for his love, grace, and tender
encouragement of all things being possible.
— *Rosemary Roberts*

Contents

PART ONE

THE PATH
OF ZEN

CHAPTER ONE

DEFINING THE INDEFINABLE

What in the universe is Zen?
Where in the world did Zen come from?

Much has been written—as well as analyzed, intellectualized, debated, elevated, dictated, and contradicted—about what, exactly, Zen is. Is it a religion? Psychology? Mysticism? Philosophy? A spiritual practice? An altered state? The way to inner and global peace? The answer is both yes and no. Zen is all those things, sort of, and none of them, essentially.

Zen is said to be "beyond doctrine, beyond words." Yet, all branches of Buddhism, including Zen, trace back to some ten thousand scriptures (sutras) that are regarded as the written record of the teachings of Buddha, the founding father of Buddhism. Zen claims no symbols, no icons, no formal religious dogma, no metaphysics. Yet, ritual, ceremony, and symbolism—from light and water, to flowers and trees, to colors and circles, to chakras and mantras, to sermons and fellowships—are very much a part of the tradition.

A fundamental Zen principle is that liberation from suffering comes from perceiving with your own mind your true nature and the true nature of the universe, and then manifesting this deep understanding of reality in your daily life. Yet, for centuries, Zen remained the exclusive domain of sequestered disciples, whose enlightenment depended on the mentoring and sanctioning of an ordained monk. Similar sects still exist today.

The heart of Zen—the key to deep understanding, which opens the gate to well-being—is zazen, quiet sitting. Yet, zazen can be done while sitting, standing, reclining, moving, playing, or working—in silence and solitude or with dialogue, mantras, chants, rituals, music, symbols, teachers, or loved ones. In every aspect and in every moment of life, there is zazen; there is Zen. Zen is divine reality; divine reality is you. You are Zen.

Despite the seeming double-talk (it will all make sense soon, I promise) and copious claims to the contrary, Zen is as simple and natural and as accessible and liberating as breathing. But even something as fundamental as breathing can become erratic when we feel confused, anxious, or out of our element. So, let's begin by taking a quick look at what Zen is and isn't in modern Western society, and then take a closer look at the origins and evolution of Zen.

The Japanese term *zen* derives from the Chinese character *ch'an,* which derives from the Sanskrit word *dhyana*—which literally means "meditation." Although meditation is integral and central to Zen, it's neither the all nor the end-all of Zen. The Zen term for meditation, zazen, translates from Japanese as: za, to sit quietly without moving; zen, to understand the essence of self and universe. Technically, then, Zen and zazen are one and the same, but neither term applies exclusively to spiritual awareness and meditation. Given the inadequacy of mere words to describe any spiritual concept, for the sake of clarity, Zen can be defined as a specific mind-body-spirit experience or essence; zazen, as a specific method or combination of methods for enabling that experience or essence. Because the "specifics" of Zen and zazen are many and varied, we'll get into them later, after we have a grip on the big picture.

Historically, Zen is an offshoot of Mahayana Buddhism, a dogma-free religion grounded in achieving spiritual liberation and in taking responsibility for the well-being of oneself and the world in the here and now. Neither heaven nor hell exists, only the exalted state of self-realization and the encumbered state of self-deception in our earthly lives. In Zen, the exaltation of deep understanding, or enlightenment, is neither a natural high nor a supernatural state to be induced, acquired, or bequeathed—or denied—by some higher power, external force, or fickle finger of fate. This deep understanding—and the joy, peace, and liberation it enables—is already within you. It's your "Buddha-nature." You're born with it, and it never leaves you. It is you. And it's in every animate and inanimate thing around you. That, in a nutshell, is Zen.

Zen, as it's most commonly embraced in the West and in many other parts of the world today, stems directly from the Japanese stream of Zen Buddhism. Japanese Zen falls into two main branches: Rinzai, founded by the Buddhist monk Eisai, and Soto, founded by Eisai's student, Dogen. The two Japanese Zen sects sprung directly from the last two remaining branches of Zen Buddhism in China: Lin-chi and Ts'ao-tung. Those two Chinese sects both arose during the period of Buddhism's decline in China, after a vibrant and expansive run of more than a thousand years. Buddhism made its way to China from India more than twenty-six hundred years ago.

RETURN OF THE ENLIGHTENED ONE

The seeds of Zen were planted by the sage of the Shakya tribe (Shakya-muni), the man who became known as the Buddha ("enlightened one"). Born Prince Guatarma Siddhartha in a Northern India region now known as Nepal in about 500 B.C., Shakya-muni wasn't a supernatural being, neither god nor shaman. He was a human being, a flesh-and-blood mortal who had faults and gifts, experienced joy and sorrow, lived and died, just like you and me. To be sure, he was considered a mystic and obviously had highly developed intuitive capabilities, but inherently, he had no more or less "mystical" power than the rest of us.

Legend has it that the prince was a sickly, sensitive, and intelligent child who began questioning the meaning of life at an early age. Raised in splendor within the royal compound, he grew to be a rather hedonistic and pampered, but no less compassionate and inquisitive, young man. He took a beautiful wife who bore him a strapping son, and he indulged in all the creature comforts and extravagances befitting a royal, including wine and wanton women. But he was haunted by the sense of something missing from his life, by the nagging sense of the existence of something more, somewhere, perhaps out there, beyond the palatial walls. So, when he reached his early twenties, he hatched a plan to escape the confines of the palace. (Sound familiar?)

His father, the king, caught wind of the plan and wishing to protect his sensitive son from life's harsh realities, intervened. He arranged to send Shakya-muni on three pleasure excursions, and ordered all the good people of the kingdom to line the roads in festive welcome and all the afflicted people to stay out of sight. At least, that was the plan.

On the first excursion, a decrepit old man suddenly appeared in the prince's line of vision. On the second pleasure trip, the prince encountered a man addled with disease. On the third outing, a corpse was laid in his path. Having never before seen the impairments of age, the ravages of illness, and the brutality of death, Shakya-muni was horrified and terrified at the thought of his own impending doom, and he was overcome with grief and concern for the aged, sick, and dying. Greatly distressed, Shakya-muni withdrew to the palace, abstained from sensual pleasures, and stewed on his rude awakening. "How can I enjoy life when the fearsome shadows of age, disease, and death hover nearby?" he raged. "Because death is the inevitable fixed end, what purpose, what value, what joy, then, has life? How can the many indulge and rejoice, taking no heed and no action for those who suffer? How can I simply return to the palace of plenty and turn my back on the suffering outside its walls?"

Oh, but the universe is wise. You see, as the myth goes, the Gods of the Pure Abode intended for Shakya-muni to experience both pleasure and suffering. Why? Because both are necessary for enlightenment, and Shakya-muni was predestined to be a Buddha, a "fully enlightened one." Of course, our boy Shak hadn't figured that out yet. As it turns out, according to Buddhist cosmology, Shakya-muni himself had decided eons before—in a previous life while under the tutelage of his predecessor, Dipankara—to reincarnate as the twenty-fifth Buddha sometime between 3000 B.C. and 3000 A.D. Orthodox Buddhists believe that Buddhas are born on Earth at appropriate intervals, sort of on an as-needed basis when too many humans have strayed too far from spiritual reality. Technically, then, the sutras (Buddhist scriptures) attributed to the Buddha aren't merely the record of one man's teachings, but more precisely, they're the representation of an infinite and universal spiritual knowledge.

This is a good time to note that the teachings of Shakya-muni were transmitted orally for more than five hundred years. During a three-hundred-year period that began six hundred years after the Buddha's death, his teachings—the sutras ("thread of strung jewels")—were finally recorded in Pali by Hinayana and in Sanskrit by Mahayana Buddhist monks. Both canons have since been translated in full or in part thousands of times in numerous languages. Originally, there were reportedly more than ten thousand sutras. Some are now missing, and only a few have been translated into English.

Zen derives most directly from the Mahayana scriptures, but borrows and adapts sutras from the thousands of canons now in existence—and adheres to no set doctrine. Now, let's return to the tale of the prince of Shakya, and the long and winding road to Zen.

After glimpsing the dire triad of age, illness, and death, the prince grew increasingly discontent. At age 29, no longer able to sit on his duff eating grapes from the lips of lovelies while the world writhed in pain, he set out on the proverbial quest to find himself and a way to relieve suffering. First he turned to the Brahmans, practitioners of extreme contortionist Yoga meditation and abstinence from sustenance. He studied for six years with many teachers and then began the life of a wandering monk, adhering to the self-castigating practices of a yogi. Starving and near death—but no closer to liberation—he finally took nourishment, which caused the abrupt departure of five fellow ascetic companions. Shakya-muni took refuge under a bodhi tree, vowing not to stand until he attained the wisdom to end all suffering. He sat all day and through the night meditating, just sitting quietly, letting his thoughts wander in and out of his mind.

At the break of dawn, it came to him: The aha! moment of a lifetime, of an eon, of eternity! The profound illumination of the "Wise and Enlightened One," the Buddha!

So, what was this grand revelation, which Shakya-muni pronounced forty-nine days later to his estranged fellow monks? (Only one of whom "got" it, by the way.) At his great sermon at Deer Park, the Buddha laid out the three pivots on which the wheel of dharma—the way of understanding and love to alleviate all suffering—revolves:

The Middle Way. Enlightenment, true liberation of the spirit, doesn't come from twisting oneself into a pretzel, nor does it come from saturating one's physical senses. It comes from a meditative practice midway between ascetic and sloth, from balancing a still body with a quiet mind, from a center point at which opposing sides are of equal distance and distribution. In other words, if you destroy your mental or physical health—whether by self-deprivation or self-indulgence—you won't have the wherewithal to awaken your spirit so that you might relieve your own suffering, much less that of others.

The Four Noble Truths. Spiritual liberation is possible only by recognizing the existence of suffering, the causes of suffering, the possibility of well-being, and the source of well-being. It also requires abiding by these holy truths in a tangible way. In the words of The Buddha, "Suffering must be comprehended, its cause given up, its stopping mastered, and this path developed."

The Eightfold Path. According to The Buddha, the path of enlightenment—which leads to and arises from the middle way and the four noble truths, which are also integral to one another—consists of embodying eight essential ideals in our daily lives: right view, right thought, right speech, right action, right livelihood, right effort, right mindfulness, and right concentration.

This sermon, the Buddha's first "dharma talk," was recorded five hundred years later as the Turning of the Wheel of Dharma sutra. It remains the root of all branches of Buddhism, including Zen. In Chapter 2, Zen Spirit, we'll take a closer look at the Middle Way, the Four Noble Truths, and the Eightfold Path.

The Buddha practiced his quiet sitting and teaching, while living homeless in the middle of a remote forest for forty-nine years. During this period, he was appointed Shakya-muni ("Sage [muni] of Shakya") and was also called Kshantivadin ("preacher of patience") by the people. Before his death, Shakya-muni handed down the dharma "mind seal" to an enlightened follower, Mahakashyapa, who handed it down to Ananda, and on down the line it went to the twenty-eighth patriarch of Indian Buddhism, Bodhidharma (a.k.a. Dharma).

A Buddha grows in India

In the history of Buddhism, Bodhidharma (Dharma) ranks second only to the Buddha. Much of the acclaim stems from his famous nine-year stint of sitting cross-legged gazing at a blank wall until his legs withered beneath him and his mind expanded with enlightenment. Wall-gazing became a meditation practice peculiar to the Zen sect. Dharma also restored to the tradition the compassion, outreach, and good humor—the "face breaking into laughter"—exhibited by the original Buddha, Shakya-muni. These traits later became hallmarks of Zen. But Dharma's greatest contribution is simply that he transported Buddhism from India, where it was floundering, to China, where it quickly took hold, thrived in the soil of a society made fertile by Taoist folklore, and sprouted numerous distinctively Zen features.

For sixty years, Bodhidharma struggled incessantly with the Heterodox Buddhist stream (southern) in India. When his predecessor, Prajnatara, conveyed the buddha "mind seal" to Bodhidharma, he advised him to leave India and establish a Buddhist mission in China. Soon after Prajnatara's death, Dharma sailed north to China, where he became the First Patriarch of Chinese Buddhism in the sixth century a.d.

Bodhidharma's forty-year reign as the First Patriarch of Chinese Buddhism launched a rapid, five-hundred-year expansion in China. After the death of the Fifth Patriarch, Chinese Buddhism split into two streams. The northern sect adhered to the diligent study of scriptures. The southern sect—under the leadership of the last and Sixth Chinese Patriarch, Hui-neng—centered on transcendental enlightenment. All of Bodhidharma's five successors, but particularly Hui-neng, contributed or elaborated several precepts that are distinctively Zen, including:

- **The penetrating wisdom of silence**
- **Meditating in daily activities**
- **The transitory nature of all things**
- **The oneness of all beings**
- **The mastery of meditation**
- **The focus on insight rather than on scripture.**

Hui-neng, who became a monk as a grown man in 676 and advanced the Buddhist doctrine until his death in 713, is credited with being the true founder of Chinese Zen. One of his most influential and enduring insights was of the mirror-like relationship between mind and reality. He also taught that meditation isn't a means to an end, not apart from and thus induced to "get" enlightenment. Contemplation and enlightenment are one and the same—"inseparable, as the lamp is to its light." Hui-neng further believed that seeing deeply into our mirror-minds requires the absence of all desires, expectations, thoughts, and images.

Hui-neng taught that we must return to our original self-nature, which is free from duality—devoid of such separators as here and there, blue and yellow, round and square, plant and animal, mind and body, you and me. We need only to steady our inward gaze and look directly into our mirror-minds to reveal our true nature, which is buddha-nature—the "perfect" essence of all sentient (animate) and insentient (inanimate) existence.

These insights, articulated more than two thousand years ago, remain at the core of Zen today.

THE GOLDEN AGE OF CHINESE ZEN

The one hundred years after Hui-neng's death were the zenith of Chinese Zen. Innumerable verses, parables, scriptures, rituals, and ceremonies derived from this era. One of the enduring principles that came to light during this heyday was the importance of work.

As put forth by Zen master Pai-chang (749–814): "A day without work, a day without eating."

During this era, intense one-on-one sessions between master and disciple, characterized by senseless dialogue and absurd actions, came into practice. The gentle teacher exemplified in Shakya-muni and Bodhidharma gave way to the harsh taskmaster as exemplified by Ma-tsu (707–787). Ma-tsu was the first bodhisattva (enlightened monk, usually a teacher) to combine paradoxical dialogue with rude shouting (katsu) and physical assaults such as twisting a disciple's nose or whacking one upside the head, supposedly to bring about instantaneous enlightenment born of fatigue (to empty the mind) and shock (through insult and pain). This practice later gained prominence in Lin-chi and in Rinzai (Japan), and variations are still used in certain Zen schools today.

In 845, Emperor Wu-tsung undertook the annihilation of Buddhism in China—and nearly succeeded. By the time the "great persecution" ended, only the Zen branches in southern China still thrived. These subsequently split into separate sects, the Five

Houses, which persisted from 907 to 960. Out of this period came several classic Zen precepts and practices. One Zen insight from that time that endures today is, "Reality is now; now is every day; every day is a good day."

The use of circles to represent Zen concepts became a common practice in a few of the southern sects. For example, the doctrine of the six basic attributes of being that are neither identical nor different—namely, totality and distinction, identity and difference, becoming and passing away—was depicted within a circle. The Zen student would then contemplate the circular diagram to gain insight into the interpenetrating nature of these six attributes. Various sutras and verses also make reference to the "circle of wonder," the relaxed mind-body state that gives way to enlightenment.

The Lin-chi and Ts'ao-tung were the most powerful of the Five Houses and the only two to perpetuate. The key difference between them was that Lin-chi relied on mind bending, exchanges between teacher and student as a way to elicit enlightenment, whereas Ts'ao-tung relied on silent, "no-mind" sitting as a way to gradual enlightenment.

Another striking difference was that in Lin-chi, enlightenment required both a monastic life and the certification of a Zen master, whereas Ts'ao-tung aspired to an intuitive understanding of reality that cultivated a hear-no-evil, speak-no-evil, do-no-evil secular life. A third important distinction was the Lin-chi's total rejection of the sutras, whereas the Ts'ao-tung reinvigorated the sutras.

Lin-chi and Ts'ao-tung continued to thrive throughout the Sung period of Chinese history. Both sects held considerable political and cultural sway. Nobles and philosophers frequented the peaceful Zen temples, and Zen monks were among the eminent artists of the time. The creation and appreciation of fine art remains a trademark of Zen.

In terms of Zen principles and practices, one of the greatest lasting influences of this period is the kung-an, or koan (Japanese), the literal translation of which is "public notice." The Lin-chi took koan practice to new heights and produced several koan collections, some of which are still used today. In Zen, a master gives a student a koan, usually in the form of a paradoxical puzzle, to ponder and ostensibly to solve, but the real function of a koan is to trigger enlightenment.

Koans usually consist of a verbal anecdotal story or a short obscure statement, though pantomime and odd gestures are sometimes used.

For their part, the Ts'ao-tung perfected the art of "silent illumination." These monks also translated and expounded upon the sutras, and produced a wealth of verses (gathas), proverbs, and other literature, much of which has become part of the Zen canon.

The Chinese sect Lin-chi gave rise to the Japanese sect Rinzai, which is similarly distinguished by koan exercises (riddles) administered by and flash-enlightenment-sanctioned by a Zen master (roshi). The Chinese sect Ts'ao-tung gave rise to the Japanese sect Soto, which similarly focuses on quiet sitting (zazen) and intuitive understanding.

The migration of Zen from China to Japan occurred in the twelfth century A.D., six hundred years after its migration from India to China in the sixth century A.D. Today, Zen is extant in China, though it continues to flourish in Japan.

JAPAN: TWO STREAMS DIVERGED, ONE FLOWING EAST TO WEST

Zen sunk its roots deeply into Japanese soil and quickly blossomed once the first Chinese Zen master, Eisai, transplanted himself in Japan. The soil, of course, had already been amended with Buddhist sensibilities, beginning in the fourth century A.D., when the first Buddha statue was brought to Japan from Korea. The early Japanese Buddhist schools were infused with magic, superstition, and extremely esoteric teachings. Eisai's arrival in Japan marked a return to the "practical magic" of Zen—the commonsense application of an awakened soul's right view, right thought, and right action approach, both to spiritual and daily life.

Eisai's timing was perfect. It had been a distressing period in Japan, where political, socioeconomic, and religious strife was increasingly common. A population longing for salvation flocked to this religion of "Infinite Light and Great Compassion," as if in response to a "cry from a burning house" (Lotus Sutra). Zen also found a welcome mat among the aristocracy, the samurai and shogun, who could relate to the practical, logical simplicity of Zen.

Rinzai, the branch of Japanese Zen established by Eisai, mirrored that of his homeland sect, Lin-chi—most significantly, in terms of the sect's monastic formality, exhaustive study of sutras, and strident koan exercises. Enlightenment was hard work. It was Eisai's student, Dogen, who broke from Rinzai and infused the tradition with most of the characteristics now associated with Zen. At least one contemporary Zen practice is a carryover from Rinzai: the tea ceremony, chado (or chedo). It was Eisai who brought tea seeds from China and planted them in Japan. Meditating while focusing on or counting one's breath (shikan-taza, a form of zazen) is another ancient Zen practice carried forth from India, embellished in China, imbued in Rinzai, and still practiced among some Zen followers today.

Dogen was practicing shikan-taza when he experienced the great awakening that sent him off in his own direction. Upon hearing and heeding the master's words of guidance to "let fall body and mind," Dogen experienced a sudden awakening. Instantly, he understood his true nature and the nature of the universe. With his mind's eye fully opened, he saw the gate to understanding and beyond it the path to liberation, or freedom from suffering. Dogen's "gateway" to enlightenment was zazen—quiet sitting, nice and easy, with no goal of enlightenment or anything else, with no striving or struggling to unravel the Great Mystery. Letting go and unifying mind and body enables the soul-awakening light of reality within each person to emanate. Zazen was It, with a capital i. But it wasn't all.

Dogen articulated and perfected the art of zazen. It was central to his practice, and it was and is what distinguishes Zen from other spiritual practices that use meditation, which involves putting a thought or image into the mind, contrary to zazen, which requires emptying the mind. However, Dogen and his Soto followers also used both in-motion and motionless zazen, and continued to use koans, various forms of meditation, mantras, one-on-one discussions with a master, and other classic Zen practices. Most Zen practitioners today use at least some, if not many, of these methods—but zazen still holds the key to that blessed gate to understanding and compassion, leading to the path of personal and universal well-being.

His teachings, writings, and historical living example show Dogen to have been the quintessential humanitarian and creative thinker. Though a devout monk and disciplined in his spiritual practice, he was also genial and joyful, and dedicated not only to mentoring monks and nuns but also to doing community service. He stressed that illumination was possible for anyone, from the monk to the devout, from the educated to the commoner. These traits continue to distinguish modern bodhisattvas, those truly enlightened practitioners of Zen.

Dogen claimed that peace was possible—if people were truly enlightened and if they could achieve deep understanding, which he believed inevitably results in compassion and "loving-kindness" (good heart in action). Again, zazen held the key—provided it was done daily and properly. And so, Dogen set forth strict and concise guidelines, many of which are still used today. Probably the most important of these is having "beginner's mind"—that is, approaching not only zazen but also daily life as if you're a beginner, alert and taking it all in, learning as you go.

Like all sentient (feeling) beings, Dogen's childhood and personal life helped shape his spiritual life. Born of nobility and highly intelligent, he received a first-rate education and read his first Chinese poems at age 4. Poetry would console Dogen throughout his life, and he contributed numerous poems to the Zen canon. His love of nature, inspired and nurtured by his mother, imbued his life as well as his spiritual insights and teachings. Both poetry and nature resonate throughout Zen today.

Perhaps one of the most pivotal influences on Dogen's life was the tragic loss of his father at age 2 and his mother at age 7. The young orphan learned early the twin realities of suffering and impermanence (all things are transitory)—insights that are integral to Zen even today. On her deathbed, Dogen's mother, recognizing the purity of her son's heart, implored him to become a monk, to follow a dharma (spiritual versus material) path, and to work toward the greater good of all sentient beings. Soon after his mother's death, he fled the home of his aristocrat uncle, who intended that Dogen become his successor, and joined a younger uncle who lived as a homeless hermit enmeshed in Buddhist and esoteric spiritual practices. These influences—along with the teachings of the Zen masters before him, his inherent compassionate and inquisitive nature, and perhaps his karma—led Dogen to become the founder of the strongest Zen sect in Japanese and modern world history, and one of the greatest bodhisattvas of all time.

Interestingly, Dogen didn't set out to create a new Zen sect. His intent was merely to devote his life to furthering the notion of zazen as the gateway to intuitive wisdom and salvation. He was no self-proclaimed religious leader espousing a new and better spiritual path. In fact, he didn't even claim zazen as "his" nor that it "belonged" to any particular school of Zen. Indeed, he regarded zazen as nothing more or less than the "great way of the (ancient) Buddhas and the patriarchs." But in time, the flock of followers walking in step with Dogen far outnumbered those of the Rinzai school. And they grew in number and spread across the land, and more than six hundred years after Dogen's death, they ventured east to the West.

THE BUDDHA NEXT DOOR

During the blossoming of both the Rinzai and Soto sects in Japan, Zen spread to Korea and Vietnam. Meanwhile, myriad branches of Buddhism continued to sprout in China, Tibet, and throughout the Far East. In the nineteenth century, Zen finally made its way to the Western hemisphere, where it's often mistakenly thought of as an Asian religion (remember, it originated in India). Today, Zen is virtually nonexistent in modern China and is no longer a dominant religion in India, but it continues to flourish in Japan and has been gaining ground in Europe and North America over the last few decades.

Like all things "foreign" to the West, the gradual assimilation of Zen into Western culture has come only with adaptation and not without controversy and confusion. Some purists have considered the westernization of Zen to be the bastardization of Zen. Others flatly denounce it as not being Zen at all or as being Zen-like at best. Still others scoff that it's "Zen light" or "Yuppie Zen." Call it what you will, Zen as it's commonly embraced in the West is helping millions of people live better lives. Who can argue with that? So, I'm not going to compare "true" Zen with "homogenized" Zen. I'm not going to argue the merits or demerits of doing Zen this way or that. And I'm sure as Buddha not going to perpetuate the contention that Zen is indefinable—for the simple reason that doing so renders this highly accessible and beneficial practice inaccessible and undesirable to us "regular" people. As the psychic Edgar Cayce said, "The confused mind says no." And personally, I think the world could use a whole lot more people saying yes to Zen—which says YES, YES, YES! to life...and to mental, physical, spiritual, emotional, personal, and global well-being.

Imagine that.

Imagine a world in which you see no division, no degree of separation, between your body and mind, between you and your mate, your family, your friends, and your neighbors, next door and around the globe. Imagine no distinction between you and the pure essence of all things, sentient and nonsentient, on Earth and beyond. Imagine that your neighbor and his neighbor and her neighbor share this perception of a universally interconnected reality. Then, imagine doing harm—that is, doing anything but good—to yourself, others, or the Earth, and in so doing or not doing, harming or neglecting the universe, and so continuing the circle of suffering over and again, ad infinitum. It's unimaginable if we truly understand in the depth of our souls that everyone and everything is interconnected and the same, without labels, status, or attachment to any divisional concept or construct, of equal value, and yet transitory—an essential blip in the grand circle of life.

The way to this deep understanding is, was, and always will be zazen—getting real with yourself by delving deeply into yourself—using whatever meditation method works for you: sitting, standing, walking, talking, working, or playing, in solitude or in good company. With this deep understanding comes compassion. And with compassion comes loving-kindness. And with loving-kindness comes the healing and well-being of your own mind, body, and spirit. And then you'll have not only the compassion and loving-kindness but also the clarity and the strength of character—the "perfection of personality," in Buddha's words—to help heal and facilitate the well-being of others and the world.

That, in a nutshell, is Zen.

'Tis not so abstruse and out-of-reach, after all. Of course, the above explanation deals with basic concepts that can be explained. It doesn't attempt to define the actual nature of deep understanding— how it manifests, how it feels—which is, after all, indefinable. The only way to know satori is to experience satori.

So let's examine the basic concepts and practices of Zen, which will help unlock the gate to your own Buddha-nature and light the path to your well-being.

CHAPTER TWO

ZEN SPIRIT

Concepts and teachings

BEGINNER'S MIND

Zen at its most effective requires that you send both your "ego mind" and your "monkey mind" to the rear seat, and let your "beginner's mind" take over the driving. Ego mind is that database of ideas and opinions that program how we interface with the world. We need ego mind; it's an integral part of our being and instrumental to the daily business of living. But ego mind filters and processes everything it comes into contact with, assigning it a label and fitting it into some slot. Monkey mind is ego mind run amok, constantly chasing after whatever you desire—a new car, a raise, thinner thighs, well-behaved children, romance, or chocolate—bouncing from one thing to another. In modern life, both ego mind and monkey mind spend far too much time at the steering wheel, too often driving nonstop, 80 mph into chaos and "roboto misery."

Beginner's mind, on the other hand, is full of wonder and curiosity, like an infant. Free from preconceived notions and doubt, beginner's mind expects and judges nothing and wants only to absorb whatever floats into its wide-open consciousness. That doesn't mean, however, that beginner's mind is passive or easy to achieve or all warm and fuzzy. Quite the contrary. Beginner's mind pays close attention and sees all, even the scary and ugly stuff. It requires an urgent, almost desperate need to know who you really are and what your life really means. Despite its inherent nature, it takes practice, patience, and perseverance to coax beginner's mind out of the trunk and into the driver's seat.

The ride isn't always smooth and easy with beginner's mind at the wheel, but the view is clear and vast: like tooling along a mountain ridge on a bright summer day with the top down. With beginner's mind, you become acutely aware of the steep hills and the narrow passages—of your direction and misdirection, your strengths and weaknesses, your friends and foes.

The aim of Zen isn't to master, but rather to become a masterful student of both your meditation (which is the central practice of Zen) and your daily life. And that requires an open and inquisitive mind, a beginner's mind, that seeks not to be perfect—but to just do it!

In the beginner's mind there are many possibilities; In the expert's mind there are few.
~ SHUNRYU SUZUKI

THE MIDDLE WAY

There is a balanced approach to living and to meditating that is most conducive to well-being. The Middle Way isn't "sitting on the fence," straddling and wavering back and forth between two extremes. It's the midpoint at which two "sides" cease to be separate, when you can no longer feel the weight or see the prominence of one or the other.

In all things, the Middle Way is the third and higher midpoint between any two base poles. As in a triangle, the converging point rises above and centers the two parallel points, forming an apex. This third, higher point elevates, connects, and absorbs the disconnected pair, creating a unifying whole. From this pinnacle, reality is clear, and good judgment and appropriate action are possible.

In meditation and in daily life, the Middle Way is when mind and body work freely together, neither being restrained nor strained. It means integrating meditation into your life, and using meditation to help integrate your life. At the most basic level, the Middle Way is doing what suits you and not doing what doesn't suit you.

Another way to envision the Middle Way is as the center of a circle. No matter which way you turn it, the center remains at equal distance from any point along the exterior surface. No matter which or how many colors or shapes are on the outside of that ball, when you spin it, the colors and shapes blend together. When you bounce it, roll it, or throw it, the center remains at the center. The sphere is dynamic, but the center is still and constant.

When I find myself at either extreme of reality—jubilant or despondent—and unable to focus and sustain mindfulness, I sometimes begin meditation with a visualization exercise. I picture myself in the eye of a tornado or hurricane, floating in a void and absent of all sensory input. Once I'm calm and centered, I become intensely curious about what's going on beyond my bubble of nothingness. With my mind's eye, I stay right where I am but peer deeply through the void at all the stuff swirling around me. I see a parade of people and events with crystal clarity. I recognize them one by one and then just let them fall from view, without trying to grab hold of or being sucked away with them, yet knowing deep inside that the bubble and the swirling dervish are inseparable from one another. That is the Middle Way: the great equalizer.

BUDDHA-NATURE: THE REAL YOU

Every human being is endowed with a universal essence, or Buddha-nature, an innate wisdom and virtue. Buddha-nature shouldn't be confused with conscience, the capacity to discern right from wrong. Conscience arises from, but isn't itself, Buddha-nature. Buddha-nature is complete self-consciousness, the full knowledge and complete understanding of one's authentic self.

Buddha-nature isn't a heightened state of awareness or a superior mode of existence. You don't "develop" or "acquire" Buddha-nature; you wake it up and bring it out. Yet, to describe this essence as "energy" is also inaccurate, because Buddha-nature has no form. It doesn't ascribe to birth or death, here or there, good or bad. Buddha-nature is the same in the bumbling fool as it is in the sure-footed genius, in Mother Teresa as it is in Ted Bundy. It's the IS of all things, including you.

Buddha-nature is inherent and immutable—unchanging and eternal, existing before your birth, in every minute of your life, and after you die. Buddha-nature is always with you; it's pure and perfect; and it can't be created or conned, distorted or destroyed. However, it can be hidden beneath the debris of opinions, experiences, emotions, and other clutter that we feed our souls in the process of living. That is why one of most essential exercises of Zen is to continually ask yourself The Big Question, the first and foremost (if we're honest), most natural and nagging question of all: Who am I?

You won't get the answer from a teacher or book, from divination or any deity. You can't "get" it anywhere, because you already have it: right there, in your Buddha self. You have only to still the ripples in your mind, until it's as smooth and clear as a mountain lake on a windless, cloudless day. Look deeply into the pool of your self-conscious and see all that is reflected there. Your Buddha-nature will reveal itself, the real you. And you will see the three dharma seals, the insights that will light the path to bliss, glistening like glowing moons in the indigo sky.

What was your face before your parents' birth?
~ ZEN KOAN

THREE DHARMA SEALS: YOUR GUIDING LIGHTS

Self-realization emanates from three "perfect wisdoms," or insights:

1. Nothing lasts. Everything changes and ceases, inevitably and continually. Impermanence is the time aspect of reality.
2. You are an integral part of an interconnected universe. Everything exists because of and in relation to everything else, with no thing

apart from nor inferior or superior to any other thing, ever, under any circumstances. Nonduality is the physical aspect of reality.

3. Well-being is devoid of "labels" and judgments, attachment and desire, suffering and ecstasy. Well-being (nirvana) is the experiential aspect of reality.

All things are transitory, emerging in time and space in response to specific causes, and then ceasing when other causes take place. In other words, everything comes and goes and changes—day by day, minute by minute, nanosecond by nanosecond—in response to other things that come and go and change. This includes all sentient and non-sentient beings: plants, animals, rocks, you, me. Recognizing this universal truth of transience helps you to live more fully in the moment, having no regrets, and to get over the rough patches, knowing "this too shall pass."

The moonlight does not differ from the moon.

~ PERFECT WISDOM SUTRA

Every creation on Earth is connected to and dependent on all other beings, sentient and nonsentient. Everything you say and do—and by extension, everything you think and feel (given that the tag team Perception/Emotion leads all action)—has an immediate and continuing effect on all else, including you. Each thoughtful or careless act causes a chain-reactive loop that always remains within and returns to you. A parent's words and deeds—both nurturing and hurtful, attentive and neglectful—go with a child as he makes his way in the world, and color the parent-child relationship forevermore. Throwing noxious chemicals in your garden harms or kills the organic material in the soil, which affects the nutrient-creating critters in the soil, which affects the plants, which affects the air and soil and critters and water, which affect the plants and soil, and so on.

Thus, contrary to some beliefs, the universe isn't a bunch of diverse parts engaged in a brutal quest for survival of the fittest.

Rather, the universe is a whole that's made up of interdependent parts, all having equal value and an identical source energy, or ku). Recognizing this universal truth of "inter-being" and "nonself" helps foster personal and global well-being.

In the entire universe there are myriad forms and millions of blades of grass, and each of these forms and each blade of grass are, one by one, the entire universe.
~ DOGEN

In Zen, nirvana signifies well-being. Nirvana occurs when the concepts and constructs we hold in our minds—and the resultant contexts and connotations we hold in our hearts—go flying out the window and disappear into thin air. Defining yourself and others, comparing one thing to another—intelligence and stupidity, success and failure, fat and thin, birth and death, American and Afghan—and then "attaching" our feelings of happiness and sadness, hope and despair, love and hate, security and fear with those ideas—diminishes, distracts, and destroys.

Whatever pours forth from the mind, Possesses the nature
of the owner... . Like the dust in a dusty tunnel,
That which arises in the heart goes to rest in the heart.
~ ZEN VERSE

Nirvana isn't the absence of notions and emotions, nor does it mean denying their existence, like some simpleton or Pollyanna. It means looking them square in the eye, being fully mindful of the causes and effects of ideas and feelings in your life—and then letting them go, not allowing them to "poison" how you respond to them. Nirvana means extinguishing the devouring flames of judgment and craving with the regenerative waters of wisdom and compassion—that is, with the insights of impermanence and nonduality.

Let this triad of illumination guide you in your daily life, and it will light the path to true well-being of mind, body, and spirit within you and in the world.

LAW OF CAUSE AND EFFECT

Every action—which is defined as anything thought, said, or done—is the result of some previous action and results in a subsequent action. But that is a gross oversimplification of an essential and rather complex Zen precept. You don't need to be a Buddha to realize that bad things happen to good people and good things happen to bad people. It may seem that some folks "get away with" really awful actions, whereas others never get a break, let alone their "just rewards" for truly wonderful actions. It may even be so, if viewed from a time and space, self and other perspective.

Reality is, it sometimes takes a while, sometimes more than a lifetime, for the effect of an action to manifest. Sometimes, the person who did the good or foul deed never experiences or is aware of its effect. Sometimes, good can be transformed to bad and bad to good, depending on what happens next. In Zen, whether an action directly impacts the person who initiated the action or occurs during that person's lifetime is irrelevant, because there is no separation between self and others. It's all one continuous, interdependent whole.

Yet, what you project into the universe usually does come back to you within your lifetime, either to bite you in the bottom or kiss you on the cheek.

ONE VEHICLE

The coach bound for enlightenment is open to all people—without regard to gender, race, position, and religion. There are no fares or first-class seats, and there is no back of the bus. Everyone is welcome, because self-realization and, with it, contentment, belong to no one and are within everyone's reach.

Some people misinterpret the "one vehicle" passage in the Lotus Sutra to mean that Zen is the only viable religion. Not so. Zen is a personal path of mind-body training that neither subscribes to nor denies any religion. Whatever your religious affiliation, if any, Zen's purpose is self-realization and self-improvement, not the perpetuation of any religion.

THREE KEYS TO LIBERATION

Unlocking the door to self-knowledge and self-actualization requires three essential "qualities":

1. *Great faith*—a conviction, beyond hope and belief, beyond reason and superstition, of your own and the world's intrinsic value, oneness, and flawless essence.
2. *Great wonder*—a burning desire to understand your true nature and the meaning of life. In Zen, this is usually referred to as great "doubt," meaning intense questioning, but because many people equate doubt with skepticism, "wonder" may be a better choice.
3. *Great effort*—a commitment to strive for understanding and compassion, and to do your best. This doesn't mean strenuous effort, which can harm you and disrupt your life. It means continuous and concerted effort that fits into and improves your life—otherwise known as The Middle Way.

THREE POISONS

Allowing any of these toxins to enter your thoughts, speech, or actions can—and usually does—cause harm to you or others.

1. *Attachment*—associating a desire, expectation, objective, value, judgment, or symbolic meaning to something. This not only clouds our judgment and inhibits or muddles our actions, it's often counterproductive, causing the opposite effect we so crave.
2. *Anger*—malice, aggression, spite, violence, rage, one-upmanship are all forms of anger—and then there is being plain old mad. Anger is madness, a delusional response that defies understanding and compassion. It never resolves or restores; it only corrodes and destroys.
3. *Ignorance*—not to be confused with intellect, which is the brain's physical capacity to understand. Ignorance means a closed mind that refuses to seek, to try to understand, and to accept the whole truth of a given situation. Ignorance means being unaware, unconscious. Denial is simply ignorance wearing a blindfold; take it off!

These three poisons apply to your Zen practice as well. In other words, practice meditation for the experience of it, not with an end goal, trusting that the benefits will come (and they will). Resolve to practice regularly and comfortably, not to practice perfectly and rigidly. Let all your actions arise from intelligence, compassion, and "mindfulness"—attentively, fully in the moment, without attachment or anger.

FOUR WISDOMS: THE BOTTOM LINE

Recognizing, internalizing, and acting upon these "Four Noble Truths" will go a long way in guiding and enhancing your life:

1. *Suffering exists.* There is no denying or avoiding suffering. No one is exempt from suffering. It is part of life.
2. *Suffering is caused by attachment.* It stems from having expectations, judgments, and cravings.
3. *Suffering is not fixed.* It is transitory, and it can be alleviated.
4. *Suffering leaves when understanding and compassion enter.*

This is the soul-awakening revelation that freed the original Buddha from his suffering and enabled him to "point the finger" to the path of liberation for millions of people for thousands of years. It's the bottom line of Zen. If you contemplate this four-faceted nugget of reality until it truly makes sense to you and endeavor to apply it to your daily life, it will become the chariot that carries you, too, over life's rough patches and into the garden of well-being.

FIVE BARRIERS

Certain traits or tendencies block the path to self-realization and self-actualization:

1. Lust and envy, which distort and distract, and leave you wanting
2. Hatred, which anesthetizes, deludes, and blinds
3. Apathy, which paralyzes
4. Fear, which transforms into fight or flight, neither of which extinguishes the cause of fear and so leave you fearful
5. Cynicism, the disease of doubt, which isolates and disables

Everyone, without exception, experiences all of these from time to time. So, don't panic or condemn yourself or others when you encounter these traits within yourself or along your path. Instead, recognize them for what they are, try to discern their cause, and calmly escort them out the nearest exit, using whatever form of meditation works for you.

SIX PERSONALITIES

Every person is driven by one of six basic types of human nature, or "personalities." These modi operandi are:

1. Greed
2. Faith
3. Hate
4. Intellect
5. Delusion
6. Restlessness

The personality and physical traits associated with each of these personality types are outlined on the following pages. Meditative practices should be geared toward diffusing and countering negative traits and toward augmenting positive traits.

Note: Some types of meditation are appropriate for some types of mental illness, but others are inappropriate and can be harmful for certain conditions. People with neurobiological disorders should meditate only as directed by and only under the guidance of a qualified mental health professional (such as a psychiatrist or psychologist).

Six human personalities

Greed Personality Traits

Deceitful

Manipulative

Egotistical

Ostentatious

Opinionated

Discontented

Fickle

Materialistic

Greed Physical Traits

Graceful gait

Relaxed stance

Sleeps easily

Rises slowly

Well-groomed

Fit clothing

Eats slowly

Enjoys eating

Overeats

Stares, looks back

Faith Personality Traits

Cheerful

Honest

Guileless

Humble

Conviction

Amenable

Generous

Confident

Believes in metaphysics

Desires sacred connection

Faith Physical Traits

Graceful gait

Relaxed stance

Sleeps easily

Rises slowly

Well-groomed

Fit clothing

Fat/sweet/soft food

Eats slowly

Enjoys eating

Indulges

Stares, looks back

Intelligence Personality Traits

Attentive

Vigilant

Conscientious

Empathetic

Helpful

Diligent

Weary

Gentle

Friendly

Mindful

Practical

Impatient

Intelligence Physical Traits

Heavy gait

Stiff stance

Sleeps fitfully

Rises quickly

Meticulous

Salty/sour/ tough foods

Eats hastily, ignoring taste

Bad tastes irritate

Eats moderately

Turns away when sees fault

Hate Personality Traits

Angry

Resentful

Belittling

Envious

Mean

Arrogant

Contemptuous

Domineering

Impatient

Hate Physical Traits

Heavy gait

Stiff stance

Sleeps fitfully

Rises quickly

Meticulous

Salty/sour/tough foods

Eats hastily, ignoring taste

Bad tastes irritate

Eats moderately

Turns away when sees fault

Delusion Personality Traits	**Delusion Physical Traits**
Apathy	Clumsy gait
Inertia	Uneasy stance
Anxiety	Sprawled sleep
Worry	Sluggish arising
Confusion	Slovenly
Obstinate	Loose clothing
Tenacious	No food preferences
	Eats irregularly, distractedly
	Looks on indifferently

Restlessness Personality Traits

Unsettled
Moody
Insomnia
Distractible
Aimless
Frenetic
Unsettled
Sloppy

Restlessness Physical Traits

Clumsy gait
Uneasy stance
Sprawled sleep
Sluggish arising
Slovenly
Loose clothing
No food preferences
Eats irregularly, distractedly
Looks on indifferently

SIX PERFECTIONS

In Zen, perfection is a verb. It means "doing, or walking the talk." The Chinese character representing paramita roughly translates to "perfect realization" but more precisely depicts "crossing over to the other shore"—or, in the metaphor I used to sing to my children, "to the sunny side of the street." To get from the island of hardship and heartache to the garden of well-being requires enacting these six perfections in our daily lives:

1. *Loving-kindness.* Giving and helping are thoughtfulness and caring in action—thinking, speaking, and doing out of generosity and with loving-kindness. This means all kinds of giving, big and small: material things like food and clothing; charitable acts like volunteering your time or talents; and gifts of yourself like your knowledge, love, respect, or simply your smile. Loving-kindness means to give expecting nothing in return. However, giving freely, unattached to the desire for praise or even acknowledgment, brings profound rewards—that is, if you're sincere and patient.

2. *Patience.* It truly is a virtue. In action, patience enables you to focus on the moment at hand, whether it's attentively listening to your child telling you about his day, completing an important assignment for work, or meditating. Anxiously awaiting something can be so distracting that you end up missing it when it finally arrives, and the need for instant gratification is a bottomless pit that can never be filled.

3. *Morality.* In action, morality—that is, decency, honesty, and integrity, as demonstrated by the Ten Virtues (on page 76)—extinguishes the Five Barriers of lust, hatred, apathy, greed, and cynicism.

4. *Perseverance.* Holes-in-one happen, but rarely and almost never on a person's very first swing of the golf club. Life, like golf, takes practice. Few of us get anything right the first time. We all make mistakes. We all develop bad habits and injuries along the way. The wind doesn't always blow in our favor. Sometimes, the rules and players change, and we're in a new game altogether. In Zen, value isn't measured in points gained. What counts is that you stayed in the game and gave it your best shot.

5. *Mindfulness.* Being mindful means being simultaneously "empty-minded" and fully aware. It requires shushing the cacophony in your mind and centering your attention on whatever you are thinking, saying, doing, or experiencing in a given moment. Mindfulness opens wide the mind's eye, which in Zen means everything going on in your mind and body, heart and spirit. Screening out external and internal "noise" can be very difficult, and for most people takes concerted effort and practice. Meditation is a powerful tool for developing mindfulness. And with mindfulness comes insight.

6. *Understanding.* Wisdom is the active ingredient that arises from looking deeply and seeing clearly. To truly know yourself, someone else, or the situation at hand, you need an unobstructed view—free of the clouding, tinting, and distortion that inevitably accompany opinion, expectation, and any other notion. Only then will insight come, only then will you know and be known. To know is to understand and to understand is to accept and love unconditionally. Understanding is the force that keeps us from

harm and from harming others. It is the energy that nurtures and supports. It is the power that generates well-being.

In English, one definition of perfect is "just right." When I was growing up and would question why I had to fix my baby brother a peanut-butter sandwich or do my homework or apologize to my mother for mouthing off (a regular occurrence), my father would say, "Because it's the right thing to do." Invariably, I would protest, "But why is it the right thing?" (usually, but not always, stifling my impulse to also say, "Oh, yeah, who says so? What makes it so?"). Dad would look me in the eyes and say simply, "Just calm down and think about it." And when I did, all the whys became clear to me, and doing the "right thing" felt "just right" inside of me. These six "just-right" actions apply not only to your dealings with other sentient beings but also to how you think of, talk to, and treat yourself. If you abuse and neglect yourself, it zaps your energy and diminishes your capacity for peace and joy, which inevitably harms not only you but, by extension in your "not just right" condition, others.

These six perfections are both a cause and effect of the others. When they're all working in sync, you'll virtually hum with well-being!

EIGHTFOLD PATH TO LIBERATION

Liberation from suffering comes from adhering to the "right" way in all aspects of your life. The term *right* doesn't mean a prescribed standard imposed by some divine or arbitrary source. It means a "middle way" that is beneficial and causes no harm to you or others. The eight critical ways to well-being are:

1. Right view (perception)
2. Right thought
3. Right speech
4. Right action
5. Right livelihood
6. Right effort
7. Right mindfulness
8. Right concentration

One could easily devote a chapter, if not an entire book, to defining and describing each of these interlocking paths to well-being. Many authors have. But the "right" approach to any one of these is really based on common sense, and it's a personal call. If it benefits and causes no harm to you or to others, it's right. If it doesn't benefit or if it causes harm, it isn't right. And "others" means all others: your loved ones and complete strangers, sentient and nonsentient beings, the whole universe and everything in it.

The other important thing to consider is that all eight elements are interdependent. Each has the capacity to augment, or diminish, all others. All are equally important; none comes "first."

That said, we begin and end with right view, because it's so fundamental to Zen psychology, philosophy, and practice. Zen is a mind-body approach to living a full life, and it advocates living—inter-acting with the world, fully and constructively engaged with other people, nature, creative expression, work, and your own mind, body, and spirit. That is possible only with deep understanding, or right view. To truly understand, we must experience it, whatever it may be, or at least witness it up close and personal with eyes wide open. Having right view means understanding hunger and nourishment, birth and death, illness and health, impulse and self-discipline, confusion and clarity, ignorance and insight, prejudice and compassion, craving and contentment, pain and joy. After all, Zen isn't about floating in the clouds, out of reach of the tough stuff happening down here on Earth. It's about being real. Because being real—knowing the skinny, having right view—is where all the good stuff comes from.

Mind is the source of action.
~ DIAMOND SUTRA

TEN VIRTUES

Well-being isn't an end result. It's an idyllic but temporary condition of the mind, body, and spirit that can be continually reinforced and restored by:

1. *Living harmoniously*—with compassion and regard for all sentient and nonsentient beings, neither causing nor condoning harm
2. *Living charitably*—helping the downtrodden and distressed, seeking nothing in return
3. *Living wisely*—fully recognizing the distinction between right and wrong, reality and delusion, benevolence and malevolence
4. *Living fairly*—without prejudice or ill will toward any other
5. *Living humbly*—free from ego, without stepping on others to elevate self
6. *Living simply*—without greed or jealousy, free from attachment to material possessions or personal reward, consuming no more than is needed
7. *Living honorably*—beyond blame, without cause for regret

8. *Living productively*—endeavoring to prevent and correct wrongs, to benefit self and others, to contribute in meaningful and enjoyable ways
9. *Living faithfully*—with a hopeful heart, an open mind, and deep understanding
10. *Living joyfully*—recognizing, celebrating, and bestowing life's blessings

TEN DEPLORABLE DEEDS

Suffering is guaranteed not only for those on the receiving end of but also for those who don't refrain from these ten ignoble actions:

1. *Killing*—taking a life
2. *Stealing*—taking what isn't yours or offered freely
3. *Sexual misconduct*—promiscuity, prostitution, philandering, using sex to manipulate or to gain favor
4. *Lying*—untruthful, careless, and hurtful speech

5. *Giving and taking of drugs and alcohol*—abusing intoxicants or poisons that cloud or harm the mind or body
6. *Gossip*—faulting, blaming, slandering, petty talk
7. *Extolling self and exploiting others*
8. *Greed and envy*
9. *Violence of any kind*
10. *Superiority*—placing self or others above or separate from others or self

Although an entire discourse could be given on each of these deeds, the one having the most varied and controversial interpretations is killing. Some people take this precept to mean the taking of any sentient life under any circumstances, be it food, self-defense, abortion, retaliation, capital punishment, or war. Others make exceptions. An enormous amount has been said and written about the Zen take on killing. One consistent point of agreement on the topic is that murder, or the gratuitous taking of another human being's physical life, is bad, and it creates very bad karma.

Another important Zen perspective relating to the taking of a life is that it goes beyond the death of a physical being. It also means causing or contributing to the death of someone's spirit, including your own. A child who is horribly abused or neglected fails to thrive, fails to blossom in mind and spirit. Strangling your authentic self and keeping it locked inside until it ceases to be is another form of killing, another cause of immeasurable suffering.

Let your Buddha-nature be your guide. Take responsibility for your choices. Make amends and correct your course if you fall from grace. Don't condone the deplorable deeds of others. Speak out against them, prevent them and protect yourself and others from them to the extent possible. Trust that karma—the old law of what goes around, comes around—will take it from there. Have faith that transformation is possible—that with right view, right speech, right action, and right effort, even violence can be transformed into benevolence.

THREE TREASURES

When the way becomes blurred and the going gets tough, you can find comfort and strength in these three life-affirming actions:

1. Seek refuge in deep understanding and compassion (Buddha)
2. Seek refuge in knowledge (Dharma)
3. Seek refuge in like-minds and like-hearts (Sangha)

TEN-THOUSAND GOOD ACTIONS

Opportunities abound to help create well-being within you and in the world. By the same token, however, for every good action there is a contra-action. The choice is always yours. Zen is all about tapping into your Buddha-nature and letting it guide the ten thousand or more actions you choose every day of your life. The possibilities for doing good are endless.

LETTING GO

The concept of "letting go," although not unique to Zen, is uniquely essential to Zen and permeates all Zen ethics and practices. In Zen, letting go isn't just an attitude; it's a concerted action. And it's integral to both meditation and daily life.

The notions and emotions we attach to people, things, and events are the source of our joy and our pain, not to mention many of the harmful things in the world. Though we need intellect and feelings to function as human beings (their absence renders us mentally disabled and sociopathic), hanging on to them can cause problems. Attachment breeds jealousy, greed, guilt, cognitive dissonance, and myriad other negative results. Like the separate components of toxic mold—air, water, cellulose, spores—some feelings and thoughts might be absolutely harmless independent of one another, but when put together, they can fester into a poisonous mess. Therefore, we must let in and acknowledge our feelings and thoughts, and then we must let them go, like raindrops rolling off a leaf or seeds floating on the wind.

Besides, impermanence is a law of nature. All things, good or bad, hurtful or joyful, must pass. Clinging to them is what brings misery.

Living in the moment is what brings peace. Acknowledging and respecting whatever it is for whatever it is, and then letting it go is the only way to achieve and sustain well-being.

In reality, it's all good, because it's all part of the universe, part of you. So, if something wonderful happens to you in your life or a joyful thought comes to you during meditation, embrace it, and let it go. If something horrific happens to you or a terrible thought comes to you during meditation, give it a nod, say "This too is Buddha," and then let it go. Blow it gently away and focus on the moment directly in front of you.

CHAPTER THREE

ZEN WAY

Customs and practices

Self-realization is the primary aim of Zen, and meditation is the lighted finger that points to and illuminates this insight. Meditation is Zen Central, where the main action is, where the fuel and switches are, and where the cars come in for maintenance, refurbishment, and a little rest. Many claim that Zen is meditation, and even a specific type of meditation, zazen. Others claim that it's a rational form of mind-body training, having little or nothing to do with God, soul, or any other metaphysical phenomena.

From its inception, meditation has been and remains at the core of Zen. But Zen has also always involved artistic expression, love of nature, ritual, ceremony, symbolism, a strong humanistic underpinning, a subtle ribbon of mysticism, and a deep root in God. In fact, several sutras advocate "all forms of contemplation," with the ultimate goal being to "find rest in one thought"—mindfulness. So, whatever the focus of your contemplation, try to focus on that alone and fully.

In Zen, God is It—the indefinable, unquestionable, absolute, perfect, infinite source of all. But it's up to us, individually and collectively, to wake up the Buddha essence within each of us and to put it to good use. Meditation is one of the, if not the, best ways to do this. Meditation is an essential part of mind-body enrichment, and it's integral to any spiritual path.

Because Zen is a form of Buddhism and because Buddhism originated in India, many of the focused meditation techniques applied in modern Zen, particularly in the West (with its New Age influences), incorporate ancient Eastern mysticism practices, including yoga, numerology, mandalas, color therapy, Tarot, and astrology.

Then there's the venerable Zen tea ceremony and other rituals for celebrating and coping with life. Only quiet, motionless meditation, however, is essential to Zen. All other practices—the tea ceremonies and nature walks, the candles and incense, the chanting and drums, the yoga and solitude retreats, the gratitude and confessional rituals—are optional. The point is to just do it! If you aren't bored with your practice and if you derive tangible benefits from it, you are more likely to do it regularly and more frequently, which increases the effectiveness of your meditations and your enjoyment of them.

All these richly layered customs and practices share as their objective the realization of self and the actualization of well-being, which in turn perpetuate the ten thousand good actions in our daily lives and well-being in the world. Zen in practice is Zen in action.

MEDITATION POSTURES

Zazen—"quiet sitting"—is the stalwart backbone of Zen meditation. It's what most distinguishes Zen meditation from other meditative concentrations. Meditation is the foundation of all religion; praying, singing hymns, casting spells, and reading Tarot cards are all forms of meditation. Zazen, in its traditional form, is the only meditation that involves complete stillness of body and mind.

Though motionless zazen is vital to any Zen practice, it isn't the only type of meditation that will help awaken, steady, comfort, strengthen, and guide you. Any time you concentrate fully on something other than your thoughts, you are meditating.

There are two forms of meditative concentration (dhyana): receptive and selective. In receptive concentration, the mind is open and allows random thoughts and sensations to flow in and out freely. Though you gaze at the ground in front of you in sitting zazen, for example, you don't stare intently at it; if an ant climbs up a blade of grass or a butterfly perches on a dandelion, you acknowledge what you see, say a mental hello to the ant and butterfly, the grass and flower, and then don't think about it beyond that. With selective concentration, you tune into something in particular—your breathing or your body, a chant or an object—and hold your concentration on that activity or thing.

For example, if you're concentrating on a candle, even though you might become aware of the birds singing outside and the scent of your perfume, you don't allow these sensations to break your concentration on the candle, and you continue to focus on its flame.

You can meditate while sitting, standing, or lying down—motionless, or while walking, exercising, working, dancing, or doing just about any activity, including any of the fine arts. You can meditate in silence, or while chanting, singing, or drumming, or accompanied by soft music or rhythmic sounds. You can empty your mind and focus on nothing, or you can concentrate on your breathing, energy centers in your body, a chant, or a visual object. Some people find that tactile objects, such as meditation beads and silky cloths, help them to relax and focus. Others use scented oils or incense, or colored flags or lanterns in their meditations.

Focused meditation plays several key roles in Zen: to prime the power of concentration at the beginning of zazen, to return to mindfulness when you lose hold of it during meditation, and as an auxiliary form of meditation to add variety to and enrich your Zen practice. For many, it also has symbolic and metaphysical properties.

There are as many ways to meditate as there are stars in the universe. The type of meditation doesn't matter nearly as much as why and how you are meditating. Most people are drawn to meditation because they sense that something is missing or out of kilter in their lives. They turn to meditation seeking answers and relief from their frustrations, disappointments, anxiety, fear, pain, and exhaustion.

Meditation can deliver on all counts. It can both energize and relax.

Many people approach meditation as a strictly mental exercise. Others approach it as a mystical way to transcend suffering and to "divine" change in their lives. Then there are those who approach meditation as a way to induce a warm and fuzzy psychic "high." Zen meditation is an intensive mind-body training that turns the light inward and opens up our consciousness, and sometimes what you see there is unsettling. On the other hand, if you practice mindfulness—that is, if you look with interest at the images that pop into your conscious and then let them go without attachment—you'll have the energy and clarity to deal effectively with life's ups and downs. When done properly and regularly, meditation balances and invigorates both body and mind, and it can bring numerous benefits: It can lower blood pressure; bring peace of mind; increase stamina, contentment, and joy; and improve posture and sense of direction, among other things.

Although the most important goal of meditation is to have no goal, this Zenism can be confusing for some: "Zen claims to be a mind-body training for well-being. Isn't that a goal?" the confused ones say. "Because Zen's ultimate objective is the cessation of suffering, and all these troubles in my life are causing me to suffer, how can I resolve them if I don't think about them in meditation?" they protest. "Isn't that what meditation is for?"

The short answer is that mindfulness is the goal of meditation, and you can't achieve mindfulness if your mind is full of stuff. Therefore, you must calm your mind and body and empty your mind of ego-chatter, using whatever meditation method enables you to do that, so that understanding can rise to the surface of your conscious—and with it, the solutions and relief from suffering you seek. If having a goal motivates you to sit down (or jog through the park) and meditate, let your goal be mindfulness.

As for self-realization and well-being, those aren't goals so much as ideals. An ideal isn't something you acquire and then it's in your back pocket forevermore; it's a fluctuating energy that requires continual attention. Meditation is an excellent tool for stoking the coals of mindfulness, self-realization, and well-being.

The second critical aspect of meditation is attitude. To answer the question, "Who am I," you have to want to know the answer—and you have to have faith that meditation can help discover it. The thing about meditation is that if you do it properly and regularly, eventually you will realize tangible benefits, whether you go with the flow or resist it. But the going is much smoother when you truly want to wake up and tune in, and when you believe in the transforming power of meditation.

The third key to meditation is regular, earnest practice. A half-hearted, catch-as-catch-can approach might give you the pick-me-up you need at the moment, but it's unlikely to produce the kind of insight and energy required to truly impact your life. If you approach meditation merely as entertainment or a spiritual bandage, that's fine: Everyone needs a lift from time to time, but that's also as far as it will go. On the other hand, meditation defeats its purpose if it becomes an obsession, causes you mental or physical strife, or interferes with your relationships and life. If meditation is too rigid and strenuous, it becomes an albatross of misery. In Zen meditation, more isn't better, and practice isn't perfection. It's the Middle Way: that happy medium between sloth and zealousness.

That is why it's important to find a meditation or several meditations that feel natural and comfortable to you. It's perfectly acceptable—and, in fact, advisable—to try different meditation types, techniques, postures, and tools. If something doesn't jibe with you, improvise or try something else. Experiment with where and when you meditate, too. Be creative. This is, after all, your meditation. Just do it regularly, with an open mind and with all your heart.

The following are a few basic meditation methods to consider.

Silent, motionless meditation (zazen)

Though countless millions of people for thousands of years have found zazen to be the ideal method for achieving enlightenment, zazen certainly doesn't need to be your only or even one of your meditations, at least not initially. Most people, especially newcomers to meditation, find it difficult to sit completely still and silent, not looking at, focusing on, or thinking about anything. Zazen in its original form usually does take a concerted effort and lots of practice. Because of its enormous capacity to wake you up and tune you in, I strongly recommend that you at least try quiet sitting without focusing on your breath or an object, and then keep trying it from time to time. The eventual benefits will be well worth your effort. Otherwise, go ahead and focus on your breathing or the object of your choice.

Zazen can be practiced while sitting, standing, or reclining, while concentrating or not concentrating on your breathing. Traditionally, zazen was practiced facing a wall, but that isn't necessary and may not even be effective for you. Some people even do zazen in front of a mirror.

Whichever zazen method you use, it's important to maintain the state of body-mind most conducive to mindfulness: natural and comfortable, yet open and alert, the Middle Way between energetic and tranquil. If you are physically uncomfortable or mentally rehashing the disagreement you had with your spouse, it's virtually impossible to still your body and quiet your mind. On the other hand, you don't want to get so cozy that you fall asleep. (Of course, if you're really tired or sleep-deprived, it might be best to take a nap or get a good night's rest, and then try again.) And you certainly don't want to force your breathing or hold your breath. Forcing or gasping for breath is a sure-fire way to hold onto the very tension you're trying to rid yourself of.

Sitting

The cross-legged lotus position and the Japanese sitting position (seiza) are the traditional zazen sitting postures. Some zazen enthusiasts use the Burmese sitting position, with feet tucked snugly together near the crotch. Any of these postures are fine, if you can do them without strain. Otherwise, you can modify these postures to fit your physical condition or find another position that enables you to sit comfortably but alertly for however long you normally meditate (typically, ten to thirty minutes). You can sit on a floor mat, a low bench (foot stool), or a chair.

Whichever sitting posture you choose, it's important to sit erect—

straight but not rigid—and centered, not leaning left, right, backward, or forward. Sit as if a taut but flexible cord is attached to the top of your head and gently holding you upright. Also, your weight should be evenly distributed: if sitting, at three points, the buttocks and knees (floor) or feet (chair); if standing, between the two legs and feet; and if laying down, between the head, shoulders, and lower back.

Eyes can be opened wide, cast slightly downcast, or held barely open. It's best not to close your eyes, and you should definitely not squeeze them shut. Gaze (but not fixedly) at the floor or ground about 3 to 4 feet (0.9 to 1.2 m) directly in front of you.

The mouth should be closed, with the tip of the tongue held comfortably (don't force it) just behind the front teeth and the rest of the tongue lightly touching the roof of the mouth.

Lotus position. In full lotus position, the right foot rests on the left thigh, the left foot rests on the right thigh, and both knees touch the mat in alignment with one another. In half-lotus, one foot rests on the opposite thigh, the other foot rests on the mat under the opposite thigh, and both knees touch the mat. In quarter-lotus, each foot rests on the opposite calf—or, one foot rests on the opposite calf, the other foot rests on the mat beneath its opposite calf, and both knees touch the mat. If none of these positions are possible or comfortable for you, try crossing your calves or ankles as close to your body as possible (extending the legs too far in front of you puts excess pressure on the spine), with your knees touching or nearly touching the mat.

Before folding your legs into your preferred sitting posture, tuck a cushion under your buttocks to prop up your hips slightly higher than your knees. (Slide one-third to two-thirds of the cushion under your buttocks; don't sit squarely on top of the whole cushion.) Your hips should be slightly forward, your buttocks slightly outward, your back straight, and your stomach relaxed and slightly rounded, as if full. If you feel pressure in your lower back, rib cage, or groin, the cushion is probably too thick or tucked in too far.

The spine and neck should be erect but relaxed, neither scrunched up nor slouched. The chin should be tilted in slightly, which brings the ears parallel to the shoulders, and both the chin and nose should be aligned with the navel. Arms should drop naturally to the sides, elbows in but not pressing in. Hands can be open with palms up and resting on the upper thighs, or one hand can rest in the other with both palms up and the thumbs touching lightly, or the hand can form a loose oval with the thumbs pressed lightly together.

If during meditation you feel discomfort in your legs, reverse them. It's also okay to stretch out your legs for thirty to sixty seconds, and then return to your sitting posture. If you feel discomfort in your neck or back—and you've checked your posture to make sure you aren't tightening up or slouching over—try raising or lowering the cushion height.

Seiza posture. To get into the traditional Japanese sitting position, kneel on your mat and then lower your buttocks until they are resting (or nearly resting) on your heels. Tuck a cushion completely under your buttocks and between your heels, so that you are straddling the cushion. This supports your spine and keeps your body weight from resting solely on your heels.

Another option is to use a padded bench. The bench should be slightly higher in the back than in the front and wide enough so that your calves fit comfortably underneath the bench and between the legs. Zazen benches are 19 to 21 inches (48.5 to 53.5 cm) wide, 7 to 10 inches (18 to 25.5 cm) deep, 8 to 10 inches (20.5 to 25.5 cm) high in the back, and 6 to 8 inches (15 to 20.5 cm) high in the front. You can purchase zazen benches from meditation supply shops, or you can make your own (or have it made) from scratch or by shortening the front legs of a footstool. Make sure the seat is upholstered with sufficient padding.

Your body should be positioned as it is in cross-legged sitting: spine erect, buttocks out, full tummy; head erect, chin tucked slightly in, nose aligned with navel; arms relaxed at sides; hands resting on cushion, in lap, or on thighs.

If you feel too much pressure or discomfort on your back, neck, thighs, knees, or heels, try repositioning the cushion, or raising or lowering the cushion or bench. If it's too low, use a thicker cushion, place a second cushion on top of the first one, or add padding or secure a cushion to the bench. (A loose cushion will just slip off the bench or cause you to slip.) If the cushion or bench is too high, it can also cause discomfort; adjust as necessary to the height that feels most comfortable to you.

Chair posture. Use a sturdy, armless straight-back chair of a height that enables you to sit with your feet resting completely on the floor, toe to heel. Knees should bend at about a 90-degree angle; if your knees tilt upward, the chair is too low. Sit erect in about the middle of the seat with your feet on the floor, about shoulder-width apart and aligned with one another. Don't lean back or position your back flat against the back of the chair; your buttocks should be a few inches forward. Tuck a cushion under your buttocks, and sit as you would in lotus or seiza posture: spine and neck erect; buttocks and tummy slightly protruding; chin slightly in; nose even with navel; arms at sides; hands resting in lap. Adjust cushion height, as needed. Don't use a high or backless stool (the chair back keeps the cushion from slipping off, and your feet must sit squarely on the floor), a rocking chair, or an upholstered easy chair or recliner (too cushy; not enough spinal support).

Sitting easy. For the girl who meditated in the apple tree and the woman who now routinely meditates in the Temple of the Trees (the woods surrounding my home), I simply can't be restricted only to traditional sitting postures. Neither should you.

Though I no longer zazen in the treetops, some of my best meditations have been while sitting on a mound of moss beneath a giant fir or a blooming dogwood, sometimes cross-legged, but just as likely knees to chest, arms circling knees. I've had some great meditations up in the hayloft, with straw and an old Mexican blanket tucked under my buttocks; in the canoe, drifting on the pond or the creek; and on my favorite garden "bench"—a big old log, 4 feet (1.2 m) long, 2 feet (0.6 m) high, with a flattened "seat" in the middle that my husband carved out with a chain saw, which sits next to the grape arbor, overlooking my football field of flowers, berries, veggies, and fruit trees. Ahhh...great sitting, indeed!

My advice, which would probably raise the eyebrows of certain Zen purists, is to sit and zazen wherever and however you want to sit zazen. What matters is that the environment allows you quiet and solitude, and that you can comfortably and safely maintain a relaxed but alert meditative posture for however long you need and want to sit on it. Tree sitting, of course, isn't recommended.

Standing

I've practiced standing meditation on and off for two decades, with an extended furlough in the middle. For the first thirty years of my life, I was athletic and had great stamina and balance, strengthened by twenty years of ballet. I soon became a very busy working mother who was chronically deprived of alone time. Standing meditation, which I could do, say, alongside a Little League field or in the department store as my 13-year-old tried on no fewer than twenty outfits, was a lifesaver.

Then, multiple sclerosis (MS) appeared one day like an unexpected and unruly guest, plaguing me with recurring bouts of vertigo and muscle fatigue. This made standing meditation challenging. For years, every time I did standing meditation, I'd list to one side, fall face forward, or pitch backward. So, I quit. Then I had a particularly severe and prolonged MS exacerbation that flattened me for months. I was so dizzy and weak, I had to hold onto something stationary to get out of bed and walk from room to room. When the vertigo and fatigue finally eased up, I was determined to regain my physical health and started walking, first with a cane around the yard, and eventually without a cane around the neighborhood. One hot summer evening I made it the four blocks to the sea cliff and decided to go for a stroll on the beach. By the time I got to the bottom of the steps, though, my legs felt like they weighed a thousand pounds each and as if millions of hot needles were pricking them. I couldn't take another step, and I was afraid that if I sat down, I wouldn't be able to get back up. So, I just stood there, gazing dumbfounded out at the ocean. I don't know how long I stood there, thirty minutes, an hour, long enough for the temperature to cool several degrees, for the sun to paint the azure sky a brilliant pink, and for me to decide to quit my job before I put myself in a wheelchair or made my children orphans. I didn't list or fall once.

A few minutes later, a park ranger drove up and asked me if I was okay. "Yeah," I said. "But I can't walk. Could you give me a lift to a pay phone so I can call my daughter to come get me?" After convincing him that I didn't need an ambulance, that my Gumby legs would pass if I could just get home and get some rest, the handsome young man lifted me into his Jeep, drove me home, and carried me into my house. My teenage daughters were mortified.

Next time, I drove to the beach, walked to a quiet, secluded spot, and did standing meditation. I didn't fall. I didn't swagger. I continued my beach walks and standing meditations for several months. I figured out many things down there, staring into the mighty Pacific, setting into motion several major life changes that definitely improved and might have even saved my life. I haven't had a severe MS attack since then.

So, although sitting zazen is the standby meditation in Zen, I also swear by standing meditation.

Standing meditation, which is derived from the Chinese martial art tai chi, is at once simple and surprisingly difficult physically. Stand with your feet shoulder-length apart and even with one another, knees slightly bent. (*Caution*: If you lock your knees, you might pass out.) Wiggle your toes and feet to get a good balance; spread the toes slightly, and press the bottom of your feet gently to the ground or floor, as if webbed like a duck's.

Take one or a few stabilizing breaths. Center yourself by tilting slowly and slightly forward, then to the right, then backward, then to the left, and then straighten up. Repeat, as necessary, until you feel the center of balance in your pelvis, spine, and neck. Take one or two more stabilizing breaths. Let your arms fall naturally to the sides, allowing your hands to rest on the front of your thighs.

Keep your eyes open partially, to whatever degree you wish. Make sure you don't close them. Look out toward the horizon, with eyes cast slightly downward and your head held straight. Avoid tilting your chin up or too far down or dropping your head to either side. Alternatively, you can look at an object, such as the ocean or a beautiful painting on the wall. (My personal favorite is a photograph, by the amazing Oregon photographer Erskine Wood, of a shaft of sunlight streaming into a cave whose walls look like twisted orange taffy.)

Starting with the top of your head and working your way slowly down your trunk and limbs, let your weight fall from your body inch by inch. Take your time. Focus on the weight falling from your body, gently acknowledging and pushing away any thoughts that enter your mind. Keep your back straight, but not stiff.

Once your body is fully relaxed, slide your hands together in front of your abdomen, resting loosely with thumbs touching lightly. Remain in this stance for the rest of your meditation, or retain this stance for five to ten minutes, then slowly raise your arms to chest level, keeping hands together, thumbs touching and your arms rounded, as if hugging a tree. Hold this stance for five to ten minutes, then slowly lower your arms to the original posture. There are numerous other hand/arm postures you can use in standing position: palms up on thighs or with arms raised at chest level, arms raised overhead with palms up as if holding a great weight, arms crossed with hands gently grasping opposite elbows, and more.

As with sitting zazen, you can do standing meditation with or without concentrating on breathing, objects, or incantations.

Many practitioners of kyodo, an ancient form of archery, claim that it's a standing meditation. Perhaps it is, but most Westerners would probably consider it a martial arts form of moving or engaged meditation.

Reclining

For people with back, neck, and knee problems, arthritis, and any number of other ailments, reclining meditation is a wonderful mind-body practice. But it shouldn't be reserved only for those who are physically unable to do sitting or standing zazen. When you aren't feeling up to more strenuous zazen, lying down for a ten-minute reclining meditation can refresh you and keep you on your meditation schedule. It's also a great way to start and end the day, a pick-me-up in place of a nap, and a nice change of pace anytime.

A flat surface—such as a thick mat on the floor or ground—is best for reclining meditation, but you can do it on a firm bed, couch, or futon as well. Waterbeds, soft mattresses, recliners, and over-stuffed furniture should be avoided, because they don't offer the support and even distribution of body weight required with reclining zazen.

Lie down on your back. With your feet flat on the floor, draw your knees up until the small of your back is flat against the mat. If you'd like, you can place a cushion under your knees to support them. Square your shoulders flat against the mat, allowing your arms to fall to the sides. Place your hands on your lower abdomen, with one hand loosely holding the other and the thumbs lightly touching one another and your navel. Arrange your head on the outer edge of a thin pillow so that your neck isn't bent forward or backward; your chin should be at about a 45-degree angle from your chest and in line with your navel. Your neck should be straight, and your eyes should gaze directly upward, with the head tilting neither left nor right. Once your posture feels right, take one or a few stabilizing breaths.

As with sitting and standing zazen, you can do reclining meditation with or without concentrating on your breathing, objects, or incantations.

Focused breath

In all forms of Zen meditation, breathing is always easy and natural, never forced or exaggerated. Breathe through your lower abdomen and through the nose. Don't hold or hurry your breath. Don't try to control the depth or rhythm of your breathing. The lungs don't expand and contract at a perfectly even rate; just let your longer breaths be long and your shorter breaths be short. Most people find that focusing on their breathing helps them to relax, to screen out distractions, and to let go of their internal chatter. You can use it to focus your entire meditation, to start your meditation, or to restart it when your concentration is broken during practice.

There are two forms of breathing meditations: observed breath and counted breath. With observed breath, you simply focus on the flow of your breath as you inhale and exhale. If you'd like, you can also watch the rise and fall of your abdomen as you breath. Some people envision the air flowing in and out, sometimes as a white or pale yellow wisp.

With counted breath, you count your breaths in one of two ways: on every exhale, or on every inhale and exhale together. Count from one to ten (or to twenty), and then start over.

Optimum zazen: Guidelines and tips

Wear comfortable clothes.

Loose, seasonal garments made of a soft natural fiber are best. You don't want to be too warm or too cool, and you don't want the clothing to itch, pinch, or constrain you. It's also a good idea to remove your watch and jewelry, especially anything that dangles or jingles.

Come clean and sober.

Refrain from taking any drug—including alcohol, tobacco, and caffeine—before meditating. Meditate before your morning cup of java or tea. After smoking a cigarette, wait at least half an hour before meditating. If you want a glass of wine in the evening, wait until after your meditation.

Barefoot is better.

When possible, especially for sitting and reclining meditations, don't wear shoes or socks. If you must cover your feet, wear cotton socks or slippers with cloth or flexible soles.

Practice regularly.

Zazen in the morning, zazen in the evening, zazen at stressful times! That's a good rule of thumb, but you can zazen any time and as many times during the day, or week, that most benefits you. Meditating early in the morning will energize you. Meditating before bedtime will help you wind down and process the events of the day, clearing your mind for a good night's sleep. Meditating when you feel anxious or when you have so much going on in your life or in your mind that you can't think straight will help you get a grip and will refresh you. A great time to meditate is in the middle of a busy or sluggish day. It's amazing how much a ten-minute walking or quiet-sitting zazen at lunch can calm you down or perk you up. If you have a busy life, you might want to schedule your meditations, especially in the beginning, when the benefits might not be as apparent and consistent. With zazen, practice makes perfect.

Choose a "just right" space.

Choose a place, indoors or outdoors, where you're unlikely to be disturbed by loud noises, activity, a ringing telephone, or someone or something calling out for your attention. Your meditation space should be private, quiet, comfortable, and orderly. Other environmental factors—such as temperature, background noise, brightness, and air movement—can also help or hinder your meditation. Avoid meditating in darkness, which can be distracting and cause drowsiness.

Keep your meditation cushions ready.

For sitting and reclining zazen, you'll need a thick mat (zaniku or zabuton) and two cushions. One cushion goes under the buttocks or head; the other provides support where needed, usually the spine. The cushions can be any shape (though round is often recommended as the primary sitting cushion, or zafu), and should be 12 to 18 inches

(30.5 to 45.5 cm) round or square and 3 to 6 inches (7.5 to 15 cm) thick. The mat should be filled with 2- to 3-inch (5- to 7.5-cm) batting and should be large enough to sit cross-legged upon and to support at least your head and torso when lying down. Washable, natural-fiber coverings and fillings are best. Mats and cushions should be free from buttons, cording, ribbons, beads, and the like, and should be firm but allow some give, comfortable but not mushy or bouncy.

Stretch first.

Before getting into meditation posture, do a few minutes worth of gentle stretching exercises to loosen up your legs, arms, spine, neck, and joints. This helps prevent cramps during meditation. (Being sufficiently hydrated also helps, so drink plenty of water.)

Take your position.

Choose the meditative position that best suits you and your environment. (See Sitting, Standing, and Reclining Zazen.) Your body should be centered, erect, and relaxed. Body weight should be evenly distributed between whichever body part is in contact with the supporting surface. Proper posture creates energy; improper posture consumes energy.

Check your balance.
After assuming a sitting or standing posture, gently and slowly sway your upper body left and right without moving your hips. Breathe normally as you rock gently back and forth, starting with large motions and gradually reducing them until you find your point of balance.

Begin with stabilizing breaths.
Breathe in deeply through your nostrils and out through your mouth once or twice. Repeat, breathing in less deeply and only through the nose; repeat until you are breathing naturally, easy and steady.

Breathe naturally.

While meditating, breathe evenly through your nose with your jaw relaxed in its natural position, which is usually with the lips slightly parted. Don't clench your mouth shut, and don't force or hold your breath. If you catch yourself tightening up during meditation, focus on your breathing until you've relaxed into a natural breathing rhythm. It's also a good idea to drink a glass of water before you start so that you don't feel dehydrated or get dry mouth while meditating. (A bathroom stop is also a good idea.)

Still body and mind.

Focus on not moving and not thinking, with the understanding that it's impossible to stop your brain from thinking, just as it's impossible to stop your other vital organs from their autonomic movements. Being still means no deliberate thoughts or movements. Don't call thoughts into your mind, and don't hold them there and dwell on them. Once you begin your meditation, don't sway, rock, or pace, and try not to fidget or fret. If a fly lands on your nose, brush it off and return to stillness. If a thought pops into your mind, gently nudge it away and return to stillness.

Return to mindfulness.
Be mildly aware of your senses and the energy flowing through your body, but stay focused on your posture. Take note of each thought floating in and out of your consciousness. Recognize it with your mind's eye, without assessment or judgment, no matter how startling the thought—and then let it go.

Be quiet.
This applies both to quiet and chanting meditation. When chanting, you focus on the chant and make no other sound. Keeping quiet for ten to thirty minutes (or more, if you're so inclined to meditate longer) is more difficult than you might think. You are likely to experience thoughts during zazen that ordinarily would make you want to shout, gasp, giggle, groan, or scream. If you respond verbally (or any other way) to these thoughts during zazen, it means that you've

allowed your focus to falter and fix on that thought, and to form an opinion that you express vocally. Try to release the thought before you feel the urge to "oh no" or "aha." If a sound rises to your throat, try to suppress it; if it escapes, so be it. Either way, let it pass and return to stillness.

Fend off distractions and drowsiness.
If you're having trouble concentrating or start feeling sleepy, and you can't seem to will your focus back to your meditation, try shifting your focus to something else for a while. Focus on your breathing, count your breaths, or raise your right hand to your nostrils and feel your breaths on your skin. Concentrate on a certain part of your body—the middle of your forehead, the palm of your left hand, or your solar plexus, for example.

End the meditation gently.

Take one or a few deep cleansing breaths. For sitting and standing zazen, you might want to sway slowly and gently from side to side before ending the posture. Gently release your body from its meditative position. Stretch. If your legs are tingling or asleep, you might want to wait a minute or gently massage them before standing or walking.

The best time to end zazen is after you've attained mindfulness (complete stillness of mind and body), when you feel sufficiently refreshed and invigorated, and before you feel discomfort—all of which only you can judge. That can occur in minutes or hours. Some people use an alarm clock to restrict their meditation to a specific amount of time. If you time your meditations, invest in an alarm clock with a snooze feature and a bell-like ringer, rather than a sharp buzzer. Turn the volume to low, and set the snooze for at least three minutes. Another option is use soft instrumental music or nature sounds (radio or recorded) to signal the end of your session. (A Zen clock, which has a chime that strikes at intervals, gradually increasing in volume and frequency, is also available.)

FOCUSED BODY ENERGY
AND THE CHAKRAS

The Buddha identified thirty-two distinctive yet wholly integrated parts of the human body. He advocated that each person be mindful of both the individual and interconnected nature of each of these thirty-two aspects of the physical being and to treat the body with the same attentiveness and loving-kindness extended to the mind and spirit and to other beings. The most important of these are the chakras, the main energy centers of the human body.

For more than four thousand years, Eastern spiritual traditions have recognized seven major chakras, or "spinning wheels of energy." Chakras are described as being colored, whirling discs that are shaped like either lotus petals or spoked wheels and spin clockwise. Each chakra is "lit" with a specific color, vibrates to a specific tone, has a specific optimum speed of rotation, and has a specific number of spokes. The higher the chakra's position on the spinal column, the faster its rotation, the greater the number of spokes, and the more complex the energy center.

The seven major chakras align vertically along the front of the spine. The chakra at the top (crown) extends upward; the chakra at the bottom (base, or root) extends downward; and the five chakras in between extend both to the front and back of the body. Energy channels (nadis) connect the chakras to one another. Each chakra is associated with a major nerve plexus and endocrine gland as well as a physical, mental, and spiritual function. The universal life force is said to enter the human body through the crown chakra and move down through the other chakras, transforming into whatever energy form that center needs.

When a chakra is healthy, it spins evenly at its designated speed, its color is bright and clear, its musical chime is clear and on key, and energy flows freely from and through it. When a chakra is blocked—whether from a mental, physical, or spiritual cause—its color dulls, its spinning slows or is irregular, its tone distorts, and its energy dissipates or doesn't flow freely through the mind, body, and spirit. The person experiences some sort of suffering, perhaps an illness or discontent. A blocked chakra can also impede meditation.

Interestingly, the location of the seven chakras corresponds with actual major nerve and endocrine centers in the body.

CHAKRA	COLOR	NUMBER	ENERGY	BLOCKAGE
Root	Red	4	Physical health Base Survival Fight or flight Five senses	Fear Paranoia Defensiveness
Sacral	Orange	6	Sexuality Creativity Family	Emotional Distress Sexual Problems Family Problems
Solar Plexus	Yellow	10	Will Desire Ego/Sensitivity	Anger/Hostility Victimization Frustration
Heart	Green or Rose	12	Love Peace/Harmony Emotions Consciousness	Apathy Selfishness Bitterness Loneliness
Throat	Silvery blue	16	Judgment Communication Personality	Miscommunication Prejudice Bad Judgement
Third Eye	Indigo (deep purple-blue)	96	Intuition Awareness/Wisdom Thought Faith	Misperception Confusion Faithlessness
Crown	Purple or Violet	972	Enlightenment Purpose Balance	Psychological Problems Spiritual Disconnect

In zazen (whether sitting, standing, or reclining), you can either focus on clearing your chakras at the beginning of your meditation, or you can simply focus your whole meditation on your chakras. Either way, begin by getting settled into your preferred posture, and take one or a few stabilizing breaths. You can focus only on those chakras that you feel need cleansing or a booster, or you can focus on them all. Always focus on one chakra at a time. If you plan to do an overall chakra tune-up, it's best to start with the base and work your way up to the crown.

To clear or bolster your chakras, begin by focusing on the root chakra or whichever chakra seems fuzzy. Just breath naturally and concentrate on that area of your body. Once you're fully focused on the chakra, envision it: Observe its color and speed. Concentrate on the colored spinning wheel. Envision a beam of soft translucent light polishing the chakra as it whirls. Observe the color brightening and the spokes glistening. Concentrate on its smooth, even spinning. Observe the energy radiating out from the chakra and flowing through the energy channels to the next chakra.

Repeat until you've made your way up the spine, one chakra at a time, until you've restored the crown. Take a step back in your mind's eye, and observe all seven glowing, rainbow-colored, whirling disks. Observe the gently vibrating energy flowing in all directions, between all the chakras, through all the channels of your body, and downward from the root chakra, and upward from the crown chakra. Concentrate on your beautiful glowing body until all chakras blend into a single soft white light. Slowly shift your focus to your breathing. When you're ready, end your meditation.

CHANTING AND MANTRAS

Some people misinterpret the tenet that Zen is "beyond words and symbols" to mean that Zen practice is exclusive of words. Not so. It just means that Zen isn't dependent on words or on any single doctrine. Although the sutras, which are thought to be the teachings and sermons of Buddha, form the foundation of most Zen ethics and practices, it isn't necessary to study or recite them as part of your practice. And it's perfectly acceptable to incorporate wise words from other sources. In fact, it's encouraged. The sutras say that Buddhas, or sages, people radiating with benevolent wisdom, come into our lives when we need them, to remind us of the truth and goodness that are within each of us. These Buddhas may come into our lives as teachers, grandparents, friends, or mentors. Other Buddhas touch our lives without our actually knowing them: poets, philosophers, or those "holy writers" who are both wordsmiths and wise souls.

Another common misconception is that koans (riddles) are a form of chanting contemplation. Traditionally, koans are contemplated, but they aren't chanted. (See Contemplations: Koans and qustions, page 130.]

Chanting, which involves focusing on sounds or words, plays a central role in Zen meditation and rituals. The vocalization can be meaningless—a single-syllable sound (mantra) or a sequence of sounds (dharani). The most common mantra is Om; a common dharani is the six-syllable "om-ma-ni-pad-me-hum" (Om Mani Padme Hum, which in Sanskrit means "hail the jewel in the lotus.") The chant can also be meaningful: a Zen sutra, or any phrase that resonates with you or contains a truth you haven't yet wholly realized. Actually, mantras and dharanis, though purportedly and seemingly meaningless, do have symbolic meaning rooted in ancient Buddhist history. The incantation Om, for example, symbolizes the union of mind, body, and soul, and represents the spiritual power that derives from absolute (intuitive + intellectual) wisdom.

Chanting isn't the same as reciting. Chanting is repeatedly saying the sound or words with mindfulness, focusing on the vocalization at the deepest level of your mind. For example, if you're involved in an abusive relationship, you might say, "love is kind" over and over, focusing only on the sound of your voice, until the words flow together in a drone and penetrate your subconscious. Reciting, on the other hand, is merely saying the words out loud, one time or repeatedly, usually to help you better understand their meaning or to strengthen their meaning (affirmation). With reciting, you articulate the words in order to grasp them intellectually. With chanting, you focus on the sound and let all meaning fall away, which actually enhances intuitive knowing. Both chanting and reciting are useful exercises, and there's no reason you can't use one or the other or both, if you're so inclined.

When reciting, just say the words aloud without thinking about them. (If the passage you've selected is long or you haven't memorized it, it's okay to read it.) Articulate the words carefully and slowly, in a strong steady voice, loud enough for you to hear the words clearly. Let the words float out into the air in front of you, and then "look" at them, objectively, with your mind's eye.

When chanting, let the words or symbolic meaning fall away and focus on the sound, only the sound. Inhale naturally and on the exhale, release the sound from your diaphragm (hara) slowly and steadily in your lowest natural pitch. The hara is the area near your solar plexus, the front center of your body. You should feel a gentle, pleasant vibration in your abdomen, chest, and throat. What you're going for here is a drone, melodic but with no inflection or singsong. Some people chant to the pulse of a drumbeat or other rhythmic sound, which helps them to set and retain the desirable cadence (throbbing). These pulsing rhythms may be recorded or your own. You can also chant along with recorded chants, if you like.

When chanting and reciting, the whole body should be relaxed and balanced, comfortable but alert. Focused sound meditation can be done during sitting, standing, or reclining meditation. However, refrain from chanting mantras or affirmations while doing moving or engaged (working) meditations, because focusing on sound distracts from focus on the movement, and visa versa. Don't sway or rock. Begin and end every chanting or reciting session with one or a few stabilizing breaths.

Whether chanting or reciting, select a sound or words that resonate with you. If you're drawn to it, go with it. Don't analyze why a particular mantra or passage popped out at you. When you hear or read something and a bell goes off in your subconscious, trust that it's your innate Buddha-nature trying to wake you up. The array of potential chants and recitations is boundless: poetry, prose, and proverbs; sutras and songs; mantras and maxims; words of wisdom. The only word of caution when selecting a chant or affirmation is to avoid cliché and esoteric expressions.

MOVING MEDITATION

Focusing your attention fully on your body's movements is another form of zazen. In moving zazen, you concentrate fully and wholly on the movement: dancing, walking, martial arts, yoga, running, swimming, mountain biking, whatever. The focus is on the activity, not the outcome; on your body, not on your thoughts. You don't ride the stationary bike while reading Vogue. You don't walk zazen while walking the dog. You don't lift weights to beef up and impress the girls (or guys). You just do it to do it, and you pay undivided attention to what you're doing when you're doing it.

There is a formal walking zazen (kinhin) that is done between, before, or after sequential sitting zazen sessions. With kinhin, you walk clockwise around the room with your shoulder to the center of the room or to the altar, if you have one or if you frequent a Zen temple (zendo). Take one or a few stabilizing breaths, and then on an even exhale, take your first step. With upper body erect, head straight, eyes cast slightly downward and out several feet in front of you, and hips tucked naturally forward (not protruding in back, as in sitting posture), walk slowly and smoothly, lifting each foot completely off the ground and placing it back on the ground heel to toe. Your steps should be in sync with your breathing: one full breath (inhale and exhale) for a right step, one full breath for a left step (one, two), and so on. Walk straight, without turning or tilting your head to the right or left, and always turn to the right.

To get the most out of your regular walking zazen, just breathe and walk naturally and properly. Keep your back and neck erect, and keep your elbows, knees, and shoulders relaxed. Maintain a steady, comfortable, and controlled gait and pace. Make sure not to look at your feet or the ground directly beneath you or to tilt your chin upward. Don't worry about looking a little bit left or right, up or down. Let in whatever enters your range of vision. If the mountain to your left catches your eye, go ahead and acknowledge it. If the neighbor to your right calls out a greeting, smile and wave back.

It's okay to glance left or right, up or down, and to acknowledge the beauty that surrounds you. In fact, that's one of the joys of walking meditation: You seem to notice things you wouldn't if you were just out there blasting through a "have to" exercise regimen. Let the wonders of your world in for a quick hello, then turn your head forward and return your focus to your walking.

When walking for the purpose of meditating, it's important to do it either alone or with someone who is also meditating. Otherwise, you'll talk, and though conversation can be another golden step on the path to wisdom and well-being, it's a concentration breaker. This applies to any type of moving zazen.

Exercise that involves mind-body training—such as yoga, Pilates, and martial arts—is particularly conducive to zazen. Not only are these forms of moving meditation beneficial in their own rights, but, when practiced regularly, they also strengthen your nonmoving meditations.

Almost any noncompetitive exercise and nonteam sport can be performed as a moving zazen. To maintain the kind of mindfulness required of zazen, you must focus completely on the activity. You can't be concerned with points, winning, coaching instructions, the audience, or the actions of your teammates or opponents. However, though team and competitive sports can't be used as zazen, you can certainly apply zazen-like concentration to any physical activity—and your heightened concentration will undoubtedly improve your performance. The same is true of sports and activities you do mainly for fitness or pleasure. You don't need to do, say, aerobics or rock climbing as zazen, per se, in order to derive benefits from focusing on the physical activity, moment by moment.

The important factors are that you enjoy the activity, that you're physically capable of doing it without injury or excess strain, and that conditions are such that you can fully engage your body and mind in the activity.

CONTEMPLATIONS: KOANS AND QUESTIONS

A koan is a distinctly Zen device used to stimulate contemplation. Traditionally, a koan is a baffling question, statement, or folk tale whose meaning (if there is one) is difficult (if not impossible) to decipher with the intellect. In orthodox Zen, only a master can assign a koan, for the sole purpose of frustrating the mind into submission, completely shutting down cognitive thought, and thereby triggering sudden enlightenment. The initiate might ponder the nonsensical koan for days, weeks, months, even years, returning over and again to the master to ask questions, until suddenly the meaning, not necessarily of the koan, but of the nondual nature of self and universe, becomes crystal clear.

The literal translation of koan (kung-an) is "public record." The vast collection of traditional koans are fictional, many of them metaphorical, and aren't to be confused with sutras, which are scripture (documented teachings of Buddhas). However abstruse a koan might be (and they usually are way out there), all koans speak to the essential principles and ideals of Zen. Probably the most famous Zen koan is, "What is the sound of one hand clapping?"

Contemporary koans are typically more penetrable than most ancient koans, and you don't need to have them assigned to you by a

Zen master. Again, although quiet, silent, no-thinking zazen is the backbone of Zen practice, it isn't the only way to zazen. Meditation is a great way to contemplate and "internalize" the wisdoms of respected teachers and mentors.

If during your interactions with mentors or in your readings you discover a parable, statement, or passage that catches you but you can't quite grasp its meaning, jot it down or make a mental note of it. Then, at the beginning of your meditation, form that modern-day koan in your mind. Hold it in your mind's eye until you think only of the koan. You might also want to visualize it. Then, gently let it go and turn your focus to your breath, chanting, or nothing.

Contemplative meditation is also an effective method of dealing with concerns and questions that arise in your everyday life. First, form the question or concern into a concise statement that you can hold in your mind for the first few minutes of your meditation. Once the question or concern completely dominates your thoughts, let it go.

Visualization is another useful technique when you're deeply troubled or confused. First, visualize the situation as it is. Don't try to fix the picture or to conjure up possible solutions, and try not to respond emotionally to or analyze what you've envisioned. Once you have a clear—and detached—view of whatever is troubling you, try envisioning what your life would be like without that problem, how you would feel or look, what you would be doing, and with whom. Then, let it go and turn your focus to your breathing or to nothing.

ENGAGED MEDITATION

Since ancient times, working zazen (samu) has been an integral part of Zen practice. The sutras say that manual labor is a sacred activity, that it's right action personified, and all Zen monks and disciples are required to perform manual tasks with mindfulness. Traditionally, working zazen has included gardening, cooking, housecleaning, carpentry, animal husbandry, arts, crafts (such as weaving and beading), and various other work involving body-mind concentration. Anytime you're fully engaged in an activity, completely immersed in what you're doing without thought of what's going on around you or outcome, you're doing working zazen.

Three interesting things happen when you focus your attention completely on whatever you're doing, be it driving your car, writing a letter, brushing your daughter's hair, or washing the dishes. (1) The task is performed more efficiently and more enjoyably, with fewer mistakes and better results. (2) Your body relaxes. (3) Your mind opens and expands, allowing troubles to fall away and solutions to bubble to the surface.

We'd all be a lot better off if everyone would stop multitasking and start zazening on one thing at a time! And we'd all be a lot closer to well-being if we'd stop doing things that drive us to distraction and cause suffering, and start doing more things that relieve suffering and foster well-being—at home, at work, at play, in our communities, and in the world.

IMPLEMENTS FOR GUIDED MEDITATION

With moving and engaged zazen, you focus on the action. With sitting, standing, or reclining zazen, you can focus on "nothing," on your breathing, or on a fixed object. The object may be something simple, like a candle flame or a flower vase, or symbolic, like a statue of Buddha, prayer beads, or a mandala. A symbolic object used in meditation or ritual is considered a yantra.

Yantra is more often associated with Tibetan (Tantric, or esoteric) Buddhism than with Zen Buddhism. In Tibetan Buddhism, these sacred objects are thought to convey spiritual energies. In Zen, they're used primarily as meditative implements rather than metaphysical instruments. The most common yantra used in Zen are mandalas, statues of Buddha and bodhisattvas (archetypes), prayer flags, and meditation beads. To meditate using a yantra, simply focus on the object as you would any other point of concentration.

Mandala

The word *mandala* is Sanskrit for "circle." In Zen, it also signifies "whole universe," a polygon, society, and community. A mandala is a circular diagram or form (polygon) within which are additional concentric circles, various geometric shapes, symbols, and illustrations, all revolving symmetrically around a distinctive center, or core. This visually represents the Zen notion of interdependence and wholeness: The center links to the circumference and contents of the circle (universe); the circumference and contents are determined by the center and by one another. Many mandalas also feature multiple colors, with each color representing a specific meaning.

In early Buddhism, mandalas were painted on fabric, hammered into metal, carved into wood or stone, created with fine sand ground from colored rocks, or constructed into three-dimensional geometric (often, conical) sculptures. Intricate Tibetan sand art is one form of the ancient mandala tradition. Today, mandalas can be made of virtually any natural material—wood, paper, metal, stone, stained glass, sand, ink, paint, chalk—and can even be one-, two-, or three-dimensional. (Traditionally, because orthodox Buddhists vow to protect the environment and not to kill animals, yantra made from animal hides, for example, leather and parchment paper, and plastics are discouraged.)

The mandala's center always represents Buddha (or Buddha-nature, often as a pearly white or purplish lotus blossom). In early

Buddhism, fourteen colors were typically used, and today most sand and drawn mandalas incorporate at least the eight primary colors. The design often includes graphic representations of the directions, the elements, specific animals, specific plants, various deity (bodhi-vattsas), gates, chariots, astral bodies (sun, moon, planets), and symbols for things like birth and death.

Most mandalas are created for a specific purpose, to facilitate a specific quality or energy: right mindfulness, right speech, redemption, medicine (healing body), compassion, peace, bliss, and so on. They can be simple or intricate, quite beautiful and quite mesmerizing. My beloved sister-in-law, Deborah St. Denis, a talented artist and true friend, made me a beautiful stained-glass mandala that hangs in the window of my bedroom, where I often meditate in front of it. Its colors are violet, which symbolizes wisdom, and white, which symbolizes the pure essence that is in and unifies everything. To me, this mandala represents loving-kindness and unity—the eternal connection between Debbie and me, between me and the universe.

Iconography

Statues or drawings of the Buddha and bodhisattvas ("enlightened" archetypes) are common in the meditation cubbies and altars of Zen practitioners. These icons (thankas) aren't worshipped, nor are they petitioned for divine guidance or intervention. Rather, they're intended to remind Zen practitioners of their innate Buddha-nature, and to aspire a specific attribute or inspire an action. Each bodhisattva represents a specific attribute or aspiration, and all are endowed with great love and compassion for humanity. What's more, they're ascribed specific colors.

The most widely depicted thankas are:

Buddha—Siddhartha Buddha, the "historical" (original) Buddha, Sakya-muni Gautama. Traditionally depicted as thin, sitting in lotus position, with a high chignon, simple flowing robe, no jewelry, and a serene face.

Buddha of Infinite Light—the ethereal (celestial) form of Shakya-muni. In Japanese, Amida; in Chinese, Omitofo; in Sanskrit, Amitabha.

Buddha of Supreme Wisdom—the First One or Wise One; Adi. Typically depicted in regal robes and a crown.

Buddha of Medicine—the Supreme Physician or the Healer; also the Buddha of Charity. Yaku-shi (Japanese); Yao-shi-fo (Chinese); Manla (Sanskrit). Sits in lotus position holding a medicine bowl in his right hand and a branch with fruit in his left hand.

Buddha of Mysteries—Master of Secrets, the Indestructible. Fujen (Japanese); Adi (Chinese); Samantabahadra (Sanskrit). Usually in lotus position and holding a thunderbolt.

Buddha of Supreme Intelligence—Vajrasattva. Often portrayed holding a trident rising from a lotus blossom.

Buddha of Compassion—the future Buddha; the next bodhisattva to "turn the wheel" of universal insight, when the world has forgotten the teachings of Siddhartha Buddha. Shown either sitting in lotus position or standing, wearing a stuppa crown.

Bodhisattva of Compassion—most beautiful. Kannon (Japanese); Guan Sin Yin or Kuan Yin Avalokitesvara (Sanskrit). Often depicted as a woman, with one hundred arms (to reach out and embrace everyone), and as translucent or white.

Bodhidharma—founder of Zen and father of Kung-Fu. Sometimes portrayed as wild-eyed (no doubt from nine years of staring at a wall and that sudden thunderbolt of enlightenment).

Bodhisattva of Good Judgment—savior of the Troubled; Mystery of the Earth; Master of the Six Worlds of Desire; protector of weak, children, travelers. Jizo (Japanese); Ti-Tsang (Chinese); Kshitigarbha (Sanskrit). Often shown as shaven monk walking in plain robes.

Bodhisattva of Wisdom—Monju (Japanese); Wenshu (Chinese); Manjusri (Sanskrit). Prince of Wisdom. The wandering monk who took his dharma talk on the road and ended up in Nepal. Typically depicted riding an elephant and holding a sword.

Bodhisattva of Mercy—Tara; the Saviouress (of those in danger, in pain, or suffering); goddess of boundless compassion and joy. Actually a group of twenty-one female bodhisattvas, always youthful, often bejeweled and crowned. Color sometimes used to designate attribute, or energy; for example, green Tara represents strong feminine principle; white Tara symbolizes long life and healing.

Bodhisattva of Strength—the Guardian; the Conqueror of Evil and Craving; the Thunderbolt. Vajrapani (Sanskrit); was Buddha's guardian. Always shown holding a thunderbolt.

Bodhisattva of Good Luck—king of the Northern Realm. Tamon-ten or Bishamon-ten (Japanese); Duowen (Chinese); Vajravana (Sanskrit). Associated with healing, miracles, material wealth, success.

Bodhisattva of Protection—Wei-to (Chinese). Always shown as a kind-faced warrior who leans on a sword.

Flags

Flags are another primarily Tibetan Buddhist implement, but many Zen practitioners and non-Buddhists in the West have incorporated prayer, or blessing, flags into their spiritual practices. Lung ta, the

Tibetan word for "prayer flag," literally means "wind horse." Prayer flags are traditionally flown outside (but can also be hung inside), so as to send a prayer or blessing into the wind and out to the universe.

Most people hang a string of prayer flags and periodically add more. The flags are of various colors and have symbols (or words) printed or painted on them. Prayer flags may be used to project the energies of wisdom, compassion, courage, and peace to the world. They may also be used to attract health, happiness, and harmony for yourself and your loved ones, your neighbors, friends, and even foes.

As the colors and images on the flags fade from the sun and rain, and the fabric wears and tears in the wind, the flags are kept hanging. New ones are hung next to the old and fading, just as life ebbs and flows in the universe. This symbolizes the circle of life, the transience of all things.

Beads

Many contemporary Zen devotees also use meditation beads, another tradition closely associated with Tibetan Buddhism. Prayer beads, commonly known as power beads and energy beads, have also become a pop-culture fad. In Zen, these joined strands of colored beads are called mala ("hail to jewel of lotus"). You might also hear them referred to as fozhu or ojuzu (Japanese; Mahayana Zen). Mala are primarily used either to count breaths or to focus concentration while holding them during meditation.

When used as an aid in counting breaths, the mala are typically held in the left hand and counted with the right. However, if you're left-handed or that method just doesn't feel right to you, just hold them with your right and count with your left hand. If you wish to just hold the mala during meditation, drape the strand across both palms and over your fingers (between each forefinger and thumb) so that the strand forms a loose circle around both hands.

Mala can be worn as necklaces or bracelets, to provide an as-needed reminder of whatever quality the beads signify during the course of daily living. Prayer beads can also be hung on an altar or on the wall of a meditation area. When not worn or in use, mala are often kept in special scarves, pouches, or boxes.

Mala strands typically consist of 100 to 108 beads, about 60 beads, or 21 to 27 beads, which are strung on nine common threads (symbolizing Buddha and eight bodhisattvas). Usually, 1 bead is slightly larger and shaped like a teardrop or lotus petal, and has a spherical beadon each side of it; the other beads are uniform in size and usually round. The larger lotus-shaped bead is used to start and end a meditation session.

In Zen, mala represent "bodhi seeds," the seeds of universal truths within each person from which true wisdom and insight spring. Certain colors and materials symbolize specific attributes—knowledge, compassion, strength, courage, and so on. Symbols or words representing certain virtues are also sometimes inscribed on the beads. Mala don't "give" spiritual power or conduct spiritual energy. Rather, mala serve as reminders that these qualities are part of the essential self, inspiring us to call these virtues forth and put them into action in our lives.

Beads should be made of natural materials—for example, stone, wood, metals, crystal, glass, clay, seeds, shells, or pearls. The "meanings" and contemplative purposes associated with individual materials and colors vary greatly, depending on geographic region, culture, religion, and myriad other factors. Prayer beads are an ancient tradition that crosses most cultures, and the practice has become quite complex and varied, in part owing to New Age influences in the Western hemisphere. Deciphering the wealth of information on this topic and delineating the bead materials and colors that are most authentic to Zen, historically, are daunting tasks beyond the scope of this book.

Buddhist sutras include countless references that associate Zen ethics and ideals to specific colors and substances. If you want to study the thousands upon thousands of sutras to try to come up with some kind of color or substance code for your mala, more power to you (pun intended). Because mala are used in Zen as meditative implements—and not as metaphysical instruments or conduits of whatever "healing" energies the various substances might imbue— the colors and materials of beads are inconsequential.

As a general rule, the colors associated with chakras are a good start. You may also want to stay away from beads made from plastics and other manmade resins (which release toxins into the environment) as well as ivory and other materials that cause suffering or death to animals. Beyond that, just make sure you're drawn to the color and substance, and that you don't pay more money for your mala than you can afford. Let your soul and common sense guide you.

CEREMONY AND RITUAL

Despite Zen's practical, rational-emotive orientation, ritual plays a big role. Traditionally, Zen practice includes several types of ceremonies and rituals, performed for various reasons and on specific occasions. These may take place with other practitioners in a temple, in one-on-one sessions between master and student, or alone or with loved ones in the privacy of one's home. Most Zen temples have set procedures and strict rules for performing each type of meditation. All Zen temples include an altar, and many Zen practitioners keep an altar at home.

Meditations, prayers, blessings, rituals, and ceremonies are performed for various reasons—in gratitude or in celebration, to acknowledge or to honor, to comfort or to inspire. Contrary to popular belief, Zen ritual also includes petitioning. Whereas in many religions, people "petition" a deity to give them something—guidance, relief, divine intervention—in Zen, you actually petition yourself. Ritual, then, is one method of turning the spotlight inward, to reveal the pool of energy within every sentient being. Whatever we seek—hope, courage, strength, insight, forgiveness—is already within us. Gazing upon a statue of Buddha, we see our innate Buddha-nature reflected back to us; reciting a sutra, we reflect that truth out into the world.

A ceremony or ritual always includes meditating, and might also include drumming, chanting, bells, gongs, reciting or reading of poetry or affirmations, conversations with a great teacher or a trusted friend of like mind, or sharing of sustenance. The tea ceremony (chedo) is among the most treasured of Zen customs. In chedo, the host serves a food or drink to represent each of the five tastes: bitter, sweet, sour, spicy, and salty. Each taste symbolizes an aspect of life, and chedo symbolizes the unified microcosm of all life. The tea ceremony, whether simple or elaborate, represents a spirit of harmony, mutual respect, compassion, and communion between host and guests.

MEDITATION, RITUAL, AND ALTAR PIECES

Peace, harmony, compassion, and well-being are fundamental to Zen. Whatever implements help to advance us toward those ideals can be incorporated into our meditations, exercises, rituals, and ceremonies—as long as they cause no harm or suffering to any sentient and nonsentient beings. An abiding love of art and nature has had a tremendous influence on Zen practices for centuries, and works of art and items from nature are always welcome additions to personal practice. The sutras and other Zen teachings cite countless symbols, charms, icons, and implements that can enrich the mind-body well-being practice. A few of the more common items found on Zen altars, depicted in Zen art, and used in Zen ceremonies follow.

Artwork—images and forms of nature; landscapes and animals; of Buddha and bodhisattvas

Audio recordings—of nature sounds, chanting, soft instrumental music

Clay or ceramic bowl—for "singing" bowl (rim of bowl rubbed with stick to create melodic sound, a mantra) and "begging" bowl, representing release from craving

Cloth pouch or scarf—for holding affirmation cards and prayer beads. Often decorative; preferably made of natural materials

Decorative box—called a Zushi ("traveling shrine"); for storing and carrying meditation implements; usually ornate and made of wood, paper, or metal; may be covered in cloth

Earth—shells, rocks, gemstones

Fire—candles and oil lanterns

Flowers—live, cut, dried, garlands

Incense/perfumed oils

Musical instruments—bells, horns, drums, cymbals, gong

Prayer wheel—circular, often ornate receptacle for tiny scrolls onto which are written prayers, koans, and affirmations

Trees—live, dried branches, leaves, seeds

Water—clean, clear, fragranced; fountains, ponds, natural bodies of, bowls of, artwork of

Common Zen symbols

Astrological signs—months of the year

Auspicious diagram—union of body and mind, wisdom and compassion, spiritual and worldly affairs

Begging bowl—release from craving

Bell—emptiness, penetrating wisdom, clarity

Bodhi (fig) tree—mindfulness, awakening, wisdom, insight

Carts/chariots—vehicles on path of enlightenment, leading to garden of well-being

Celestial bodies—Earth, moon, sun, stars, universe (space)

Cobra/serpent—Earth power, protection from physical harm, extinguishing of violence

Conch shell—usually white. Dharma, Buddha's teachings, right speech

Diamond—strength, indestructible faith, wisdom

Directions—north, south, east, west; also four intermediate points, zenith, and nadir

Elements—earth, air, water, fire

Elephant—Buddha rode to Earth, awakening, liberation

Gardens—floral, fauna, fruit

Gate—entrance to garden of well-being, seen from the path of enlightenment

Geometric shapes—particularly circles and polygons

Golden fish—courage, freedom, movement, action without fear, decisiveness

Golden Wheel, or Dharma Wheel—wheel of Life, transience, endless cycle of birth and rebirth; the four spokes represent the four noble truths;

the eight knobs (on circumference) or eight spokes represent the eightfold path; right action

Heart—compassion, loving-kindness, right action, honesty, integrity

Lion—courage and strength

Lotus—Buddha, enlightenment, purity, bliss, equanimity, peace, compassion

Mirror—wisdom, wholeness, unity, equality

Precious umbrella—protection, healing, and comfort from sickness, harmful forces, obstacles, unwholesome actions

Seasons—winter, spring, summer, fall

Senses—sight, sound, smell, touch, taste, intuition

Swords/daggers—cuts through monkey mind; strength, right effort, right action

Third eye—insight, integrity, authenticity

Thunderbolt—wisdom, insight, deep understanding, courage, right action

Treasure vase—longevity, wealth, prosperity, liberation from craving

Yin Yang (Chinese character)—interbeing, balance

Retreats

Sometimes, the only way to find yourself and find your way is to get away by yourself for a good dose of relaxation and reflection. Sometimes, the only place you can hush monkey mind and hone in on right mindfulness is to go someplace where there is nobody and nothing else you have to mind.

Solitary spirit-boosting, mind-awakening, body-cleansing retreats have been a traditional Zen practice since Buddha left his princely palace in search of himself and a way to end suffering. He sat himself down beneath a bodhi tree; suddenly realized that twisting himself into a pretzel, starving himself, and banging his head against the cosmos wasn't getting him anywhere; and took a sip of honey and milk, a bath, and a good long nap. And he didn't just jump upright then and there to go out and save the world. He stayed there alone for several more days, taking care of his body, mind, and soul—communing with nature—and meditating.

In Zen Buddhism, there is a formal retreat called a sesshin ("to gather the mind"), lasting two to seven days and held at facilities equipped for that purpose. Most of the time is spent in complete silence and in solitary meditation, mostly sitting zazen, with walking zazen in between to loosen the legs. There might also be chanting, lectures, chado (tea meal) ceremonies, and one-on-one consultations (mondo) with a Zen master. Meals are light and simple; sleep is minimal. Sesshins are intensive, and rules are strictly enforced, so they're recommended only to experienced zazen practitioners who want to delve more deeply into the Zen religion, and they should start out short.

For those who are content to simply incorporate Zen meditation and ethics into their lives, solitary retreats to any quiet place that is away from the hustle and bustle of daily life are recommended. Remote locations surrounded by nature—in the forest, on the beach, in the dessert, on a mountain—with no phones, televisions, stereos, or any other such distractions are also good. (You may, however, want to bring your laptop so you can do writing or working meditation.) It's best to go alone or with a companion whose purpose is also a contemplative retreat. The more silence, solitude, and time spent meditating, the better. Remember: Every meditation doesn't need to be silent sitting zazen; you can also do guided, chanting, moving, and engaged meditation. But make sure to get in as much quiet sitting zazen as you can. Also remember: You don't have to sit inside on the floor in lotus position. You can zazen anywhere, indoors or in nature.

A three-day retreat is the recommended minimum; a week is ideal. It usually takes me a good forty-eight hours to unwind, and it isn't until the third day that I am totally relaxed and alert and can sustain my meditative state for an entire day. I usually schedule nine-day retreats over two full weekends. Most of us wait until we are completely depleted to "get away" for a while to regroup. It's better to go on a contemplative retreat before you've reached that point. Otherwise, you can spend most of your time just getting rested and relaxed enough to meditate. If you're on the verge of collapse or you've already hit the wall, schedule a retreat for yourself. It doesn't have to be fancy. You can just go camping for a few days or take a three-day weekend at home alone, tending to nothing and no one, not answering the phone or e-mail, just relaxing, nurturing (but not coddling) yourself, and meditating.

PART TWO

LIVING ZEN

Living the path of Zen requires an open, aware, and honest heart that respects not only yourself but also everyone and everything around you. Of course that's easier said than done in an age of technological hyperspeed, where getting ahead and staying ahead (either at home or at the office) often imposes upon our ability to acknowledge our own breath and our own presence, not to mention that of others. How often do we say to our spouses, children, and coworkers, "I'm sorry. Did you say something?"

The point is, of course, that life isn't to be lived from a position of "getting ahead," but instead from a position of getting "it" fully. If what you do today brings you irritation, frustration, or angst or leaves you little time to engage with and enjoy those closest to you, then your goals of "getting ahead" are a continuation of the ever-popular illusion that it's tomorrow that counts—an empty illusion at best that can never be achieved, for tomorrow knows nothing of today. To provide for your children's college fund tomorrow at the cost of being absent from their lives today comes at a cost that can never be recouped. Divesting in close relationships in the present for the sake of life's future investments will only leave a heart bank empty on all accounts.

Although the steps to a happier and more fulfilled life are easy to discern, follow-through and mindfulness can be a challenge initially. The following tips are meant to illustrate the simple ways in which Zen can be incorporated and can play a beneficial role in your everyday life and relationships, from family and friends to work and play. After all, in every situation, by giving of your true self you're also giving to your true self, growing stronger, happier, and more assured that your journey is a purposeful one. Live with great faith, wonder, and effort. This is the path of Zen.

LOVE

Visualize your ideal love relationship.

First, silently concentrate on or chant the mantra, "Loving relationship," until the words fade into an indistinct drone. Then visualize yourself in a loving relationship. What are you doing? Where are you? What does it look like? How are you interacting with one another? How are you expressing your love to and caring for one another? What does it feel like? What is present in your vision that is absent in your life today? What is absent from your vision that is present in your life today?

We cannot control whom we fall in love with, only what we do about it.

~ ALBERT LLOYD SELL

Clear the dust from the reflection you project to your lover.

Are you hiding or falsifying something about yourself? When you conceal your true self or a transgression, it not only undermines the relationship but also erodes your well-being. Look into a mirror and say aloud the truth or untruth you've been withholding. Meditate, focusing on ways in which you might remove the mask. Look again into the mirror, state the truth or untruth again, and blow it away. Then, immediately show your lover your authentic face, in words, actions, or both.

The most important thing in life is to learn how to give out love, and to let it come in.

~ MORRIE SCHWARTZ

Take a do nothing break with your lover.

Block out an afternoon, or better yet a full twenty-four hours, to do nothing but be with your lover. Make it a day of complete leisure— no cooking, cleaning, parenting, socializing, working, shopping, strenuous exercise, trying to solve problems, or doing anything else that might distract you. Whatever you do (or don't do), do it together and focus on one another.

What's terrible is to pretend that the second-rate is first rate. To pretend that you don't need love when you do.

~ DORIS LESSING

Give your lover the gift of mindfulness.

In all of your interactions with your lover, be fully engaged in what is being said or done, and nothing else. When your lover is telling you about his day or sharing her thoughts, turn off the television and put down the newspaper, stop filing your nails and eating popcorn, look into his or her eyes and take his or her hand, and listen. When you argue, just argue. When you dance, just dance. When you kiss, just kiss.

Married couples tell each other a thousand things without speech.
~ CHINESE PROVERB

Color your love with the colors of your heart.
Gold, green, and rose are the colors of the heart chakra and represent unconditional love. Paint your bedroom walls rose. Greet your lover wearing something green made of a soft natural fiber, like silk or combed cotton. Light twelve golden candles for an intimate dinner or heart-to-heart talk. Give your lover a bouquet of flowers in the color of your heart. When you two are having troubled times, meditate and visualize a soft green or rose or gold light flowing through your veins and soothing your aching or angry heart.

Love is the extremely difficult realization that something other than ourselves is real.
~ LOUISE MURDOCH

Set sail to grudges.

Carrying around anger, hurt, and resentment (which nearly always travel together) about something from the past—even if only in an overnight bag—spoils today and poisons tomorrow. Some things really are intolerable and only right action can resolve them. Regardless, you must let go of the emotions and expectations you've attached to the issue, send them on a permanent vacation, to restore not only your own well-being but also the relationship's. Take a walk outside, concentrating only on your movement and breathing. Once your mind is still and in sync with your body's movements, stop and pick up a dried leaf or dandelion. Bring the negative thought into your mind, then blow it with the dandelion into the wind or drop it with the leaf into a stream.

Love is not just caring deeply; it is, above all, understanding.
~ FRANÇOISE SAGAN

Extinguish the craving for love with self-love.

When you're feeling chronically lonely, wondering whether you'll ever find true love, or if you've been feeling chronically dissatisfied with your love relationship, look deep within for the solution to your suffering. Meditate while asking, "What am I really craving?" In reality, we never crave the object of affection; we crave the affection—the good feelings—we associate with it. Make a list of ten other things that you enjoy. Do at least one activity for yourself each day, and when doing it, engage fully without regard to outcome or reward. Your craving will diminish as your self-satisfaction increases. In the process, you might just meet the love of your life or recognize that he or she has been there all along. After all, like attracts like, and self-love attracts romantic love.

Love looks not with the eyes, but with the mind, And therefore is winged Cupid painted blind.

~ WILLIAM SHAKESPEARE

Cultivate *this too* and *just this* in your garden of love.

What are three things about your lover that irritate or trouble you? In solitude, write them down on a slip of paper. On a separate piece of paper, write down three things about your lover that you adore. In a fireproof, deep-sided container or outside in a fire pit, burn the two slips of paper, or shred them into tiny pieces. Mix the ashes (or shreds) together and bury them in the soil of a potted plant or in your garden, and then plant something you love in that pot or spot. Meditate regularly in front of the plant, which represents your lover's true unfragmented essence, while focusing on the mantras "This too" and "Just this." As you lovingly tend and enjoy your plant as it grows, so too will your awareness and appreciation of your lover's whole being grow.

Age doesn't protect you from love. But love, to some extent, protects you from age.

~ JEANNE MOREAU

Go on a picnic with your lover.

Prepare a simple, light, nutritious, and tasty meal. (You'll want to focus your energy on one another, not on digesting a heavy meal.) As in chado (tea ritual), select foods that represent different positive aspects of your relationship. Choose a spot that is peaceful, private, and pleasant. If you're able, spread a blanket and sit on the ground; otherwise, a picnic table or any arrangement that is comfortable for you both is fine. Before eating, meditate on the blessing of food, acknowledging those beings who have made it possible. After eating, lie side by side with your lover in reclining meditation posture, and while loosely holding hands, meditate on the blessings of this moment and of all the moments you share together. Concentrate on the beauty and interbeing of nature and love.

Love looks forward, hate looks back, anxiety has eyes all over its head.

~ MIGNON MCLAUGHLIN

Uncover and let go of past mistakes.

Unhealthy behaviors in love relationships are often habitual, and they usually come from a fractured heart. To heal these fissures, alternate and repeat these three meditations over a period of time.

1. Holding the seed, "What are the three biggest mistakes I've made in love?" in your mind, practice a quiet sitting meditation, allowing these realities to arise. However uncomfortable they might be, don't try to silence, rationalize, or respond to them; be aware of them but then let them go.

2. For each unhealthy love habit, write an affirmation for a healthier correlate. For example, if you've been judgmental, the affirmation might be, "My love is unconditional." Make an affirmation card and carry it in your pocket, taking it out throughout the day, or post it in a place where you'll see it frequently. Every time you see the affirmation, focus fully on it for a minute.

3. Begin a quiet sitting meditation. Once your mind-body is completely still, focus on the gentle rise and fall of the left side of your chest. Envision a scar on your heart; focus on it. Envision a soft golden light

whirling over your heart, gently healing the scar of past mistakes, hurts, and fears.

In any [love] triangle, who is the betrayer, who the unseen rival, and who the humiliated lover? Oneself, oneself, and no one but oneself!

~ ERICA JONG

Go on a journey of discovery with your lover.

Learn about something new together, and in the process learn something new about one another. Take a class, visit a museum, explore a place you've never been before, read about a topic you know little about, try a new cuisine, share a secret passion, or take up a new hobby. Suspend judgment. Experience it together. Talk about it. Everything changes, and everything is interrelated. The more you discover about what's going on out there, the better you'll understand what's going on in here, within your relationship and within yourself. With greater knowledge comes greater understanding, which leads to deeper appreciation and intimacy.

Give wings to expectations.

Make a list of the things you expect from your lover or your love relationship. With these expectations seeded in your mind, meditate. (Moving meditation, such as walking, is especially helpful when contemplating a complex or long list.) Afterward, jot down in your journal any points of clarity or confusion that arose during meditation. Repeat, as necessary, until you're clear about what you are and aren't willing to accept about your lover and your relationship. Do a quiet sitting meditation. Once your mind-body is still, call each expectation into your mind's eye, one by one, and envision it as a feather floating in the air before you, and then gently blow it away. This will help you determine what can and can't be done to improve your relationship, and will help you let go of expectations, which cause only suffering.

Doubt that the stars are fire, doubt that the sun doth move, doubt truth to be a liar, but never doubt that I love.

~ WILLIAM SHAKESPEARE

Set aside time to talk with your lover, and then listen fully.

Don't wait until there is a problem or distance between you; take time regularly for candid, but respectful, discussion. Choose a time and place where the two of you can be alone, undistracted, and comfortable. Approach your talk as a special time to share with, not dump on, one another. Practice right speech, taking extra care to say nothing critical or malicious. Look at your lover, and listen fully to what is both said and unsaid. Pay attention to facial and body expressions. Silences speak, too. What is your lover saying by saying nothing? What is he or she holding back? Why? It's a good idea to do quiet meditation to center yourself and "gather your thoughts" before engaging in an intimate conversation, and to do quiet meditation afterward to more fully assimilate the exchange.

And what do all the great words come to in the end, but that?—I love you—I am at rest with you—I have come home.

~ DOROTHY L. SAYERS

Make a loving-kindness anniversary calendar.

Just as there are 50 ways to leave your lover, there are 550 ways to love your lover. A loving-kindness is simply a thoughtful thing you do for another person—also known as a "honey-do." No loving-kindness is too great or small, and all express your respect, appreciation, and affection for your lover. The most powerful loving-kindness is the gift of yourself—your time and attention. On a calendar, write down a different honey-do for each month of the year, on the day you recognize as your relationship anniversary (or on any day you choose). Then, in the true Zen way, just do it—and enjoy it fully!

Who travels for love finds a thousand miles not longer than one.
~ JAPANESE PROVERB

Go on a stillness retreat with your lover.

The objective here isn't necessarily to be idle but to be still—free of external distractions. This will help each of you to be your most authentic self with one another, and will help restore or strengthen the wholeness of your relationship. Go away somewhere together, just the two of you, for three to ten days. Choose a comfortable place, where you'll have plenty of quiet and alone time. Rent a beach bungalow, pitch a tent in the forest, borrow a friend's lakeside cabin, or stay in a nice hotel or a quaint bed-and-breakfast. Focus on yourselves and each other, not on a jam-packed itinerary. Eat healthy, enjoyable, light meals. Spend time meditating, talking, bathing, making love, and doing mutually enjoyable activities that involve only the two of you. If you start getting on each other's nerves, take solitary minibreaks from one another, meditate separately, and then come together again.

Love has reasons which reason cannot understand.
~ BLAISE PASCAL

See the reflection in your lover's eyes.

If you view yourself in a negative or inflated way, it can distort the image you project and receive back from your lover, causing both of you to respond negatively to an inauthentic—and often unfavorable—reflection of you. Begin a quiet meditation; once your mind-body is still, envision a large mirror hanging before you. Envision the reflection of you engaged in a typical or recent interaction with your lover. What are you saying? What are your facial expressions and body language saying? Are you reflecting your true self and your true feelings for your lover? Allow the vision to dissipate. Continue looking at the mirror with your mind's eye and envision the reflection of your authentic self, expressing your genuine feelings for your lover.

To fear love is to fear life.
~ BERTRAND RUSSELL

Pursue a passion.
Everyone is passionate about at least one thing, be it photography, gardening, auto racing, poetry, rock climbing, cooking, collecting Elvis memorabilia, or whatever. Engaging fully in something is a form of meditation that generates self-love and fulfillment. It also puts you

in a position, both physically and psychologically, to meet someone with similar interests. Cease looking for love, and discover love.

Do something goofy with your lover.
Plan goofiness, if you must, but if you get an urge to tickle your lover's funny bone, go for it. Spontaneous goofiness is a meditation art unto itself. Laughter has an amazing power: It can make two people drop their masks, revealing their true selves, and bring them to mindfulness, centering them fully in the moment—simultaneously and instantly.

Boredom is simply a lack of attention.
~ CHRISTOPHER FREMANTLE

Give yourself a litmus test for lust.
Is it love, is it love, is it love that you're feeling? Or is it lust? Oh, if only there was a litmus test for lust, the great destroyer of relationships and lives. In a litmus test, what already exists is revealed when

it comes into contact with a clarifying agent. In love, the clarifying agent is your own truth. At the start of a quiet meditation, form this question in your mind: If your lover could no longer give you anything—neither material possession nor physical attention—what would your lover give you?

Begin with the end.

Begin a quiet meditation by envisioning that this is the last week of your life and that you're without a "significant other," not even having one in sight. Go deeply into the meditation, until your mind-body is completely still. Then, visualize you're waking up on the first dawn of your last week on Earth and going about your day: What do you notice about your environment? What are you doing? Who are you with? Then, do that, and trust that love will come.

Get ready for love.

Before lovemaking or an intimate evening with your lover, practice moving meditation (for example, yoga or walking), which relieves stress and increases the body's production of endorphins. Emptying the clutter from your mind, heart, and soul freshens you for a special evening of sharing and pleasure.

Love comes from companionship.
~ BUDDHA

Express your love frequently.
Reach out to your lover now—right now and every day in simple and personal ways. Call at work just to say "I love you." Put a candy kiss on their pillow. Go over and give them a hug. Don't wait for a crisis or until it's too late.

Meditate on an absent lover's well-being.
When your lover is away from you, look at his or her picture, and then meditate, releasing good thoughts about that person into the universe.

The memories of long love gather like drifting snow, poignant as the mandarin ducks who float side by side in sleep.

~ LADY MURASAKI

Break down barriers.

Sometimes, an invisible but seemingly impenetrable barrier builds up between a couple. Remove the first brick in the wall separating you and your lover, which can be as simple as touching your partner's hand or as difficult as initiating the resolution of a long-standing conflict. One by one, remove all of the hurts, misunderstandings, and obstacles that block intimacy. The wall may not come down quickly or easily, but with love and effort, it will come down.

Love speaks even when the lips are closed.

~ UNKNOWN

Create something together.

Get creative! Do something constructive or creative together: Plant a garden, build a birdhouse, paint a room, write a love sonnet. As you create side by side, be together in the moment.

Love cannot survive if you just give it scraps of yourself, scraps of your time, scraps of your thoughts.

~ MARY O'HARA

Surround yourself with affirmation cards of love.

Make several affirmation cards. Place them around your home, in places where you'll see them frequently and in out-of-the-way places where you'll find them when you aren't expecting to. When you come across a card, stop what you're doing, and meditate on that sentiment.

Everyone wants love to follow them down their road; where is it that love wants to go?

~ JUDY GRAHN

To be in love is to touch with a lighter hand.
In yourself you stretch, you are well.

~ GWENDOLYN BROOKS

If we say I love you, it may be received with doubt, for there are
times when it is hard to believe. Say I hate you, and the one spo-
ken to believes it instantly, once for all.

~ KATHERINE ANNE PORTER

Gone greed, gone guile, gone thirst, gone grudge.

~ BUDDHA

FAMILY

If you reveal your secrets to the wind you should not blame the
wind for revealing them to the trees.

~ KHALIL GIBRAN

Be grateful to your teachers.

Be grateful of the lessons, both loving and harsh, that you gain from your family of teachers. Consider them practice sessions in a loving environment for dealing with the world at large, including group and individual relationships to come.

Take steps to overcome pain.

Pick a challenging experience that involved a family member and let that thought travel to your heart. What emotion do you feel? Ask yourself, "How have I used this lesson in a positive way?" Allow your thoughts to roam freely, acknowledge them and let the emotion pass. Breathe, and acknowledge your ability to think and act with right view (understanding through experience) and to discover the good within any lesson.

If you stand straight, do not fear a crooked shadow.
~ CHINESE PROVERB

Let go of apron strings.

A close family can be supportive, but you must find your own path and be responsible first and foremost to yourself. Only through the courage of standing alone can you carve your own way, make your own mark, and find your truest purpose.

Separate yourself from the group.

Obligation is an illusion that can be destructive if acted upon without a sincere heart. Find the courage to state your discomfort of a situation, and meditate on the possible alternatives. When you separate yourself from the group, right action will surface.

Find and accept your own identity.

Finding and accepting your own identity is crucial to enlightenment. By dislodging from group labels and expectations, you free yourself to grow within. List the adjectives that describe your family (for example, strong, weak, loud, and soft), and contemplate them before quiet meditation. Let the meaning of each form an identity of yourself in your mind. How are they different from the whole? How do you use your gifts individually? As they resonate, don't judge them as good or bad, simply acknowledge them, and let them pass.

Learn more about your parents.

Aside from knowing that your parents walked 20 miles (32 km) to school (each way, with no shoes) in the snow, what else do you know about them? What do you know of their younger hearts? Ask both parents to tell you three dreams they had as children or teenagers. Inquire as to how they fostered them, or if they abandoned them, ask them why. Most important, see them in a different light, an individual light.

Observe your children's interactions with other people.

You'll often find that their innocence allows them to see past the dirty clothes of the beggar on the corner and to notice the graciousness of the beggar's "thank you." At other times, your children may be judgmental, and so you may need to set them on a path of right thought and compassion, the ways of loving-kindness for their hearts to absorb.

Though a tree be a thousand feet high, the leaves fall and return to the root.
~ CHINESE PROVERB

Make new friends of the people your family members have become. Listening to family can become like breathing, done automatically, without mindfulness. Despite years and changes, we assume that we still know them intimately, but do we? Engage fully in conversation, and avoid knee-jerk assumptions in your mind. Ask questions as if you were only a brief acquaintance, anxious to understand their heart and goals.

Make learning a family affair.
Choose a learning experience or hobby that your whole family can get involved in and share. For instance, learn sign language or a new sport, or engage in a new hobby.

Though a mother give birth to nine sons, all nine will be different.
~ CHINESE PROVERB

Be as courteous to family members as you are with strangers.
We often take advantage of family members, forgetting common politeness and courtesy. Treat family as you would anyone else, as you yourself would like to be treated.

Explore your family roots.
Family relationships and beliefs resonate from the first chakra, located at the base of your spine. Exploring your family roots can help maintain a vibrant, healthy first chakra, which can provide a sense of stability and connection and an awareness of your connection to the whole.

Meditate on the first chakra.
Imagine a taut cord (an umbilicus, per se) extending from the base of your spine down into the earth. Visualize the glow of loving white

light penetrating up from the ground, warming you as it fills your chakra with energy. As the chakra begins to spin, the white glow becomes a vibrant red with energy that will blend upward and enrich your physical and spiritual body.

When eating bamboo sprouts, remember the man who planted them.
~ CHINESE PROVERB

At the next family gathering, take a moment to appreciate the time, energy, and love spent preparing the meal.
Acknowledge that your mother's potato salad can only come from her kitchen. Appreciate the creative arrangement of your sister's finger foods and your brother's special barbecue sauce, even if he won't share the recipe.

Teach your children the art of mindfulness and sending loving-kindness through play.

Spend an afternoon blowing bubbles—slow, singular, big bubbles! As you gently blow into the bubble, send loving thoughts to a grandparent, a friend, or a sick neighbor. Do so with intention, and watch your bubble rise with your message to be carried off and released into the universe.

Speaking one's mind, after all, does not necessarily mean one is in touch with the truth or even with the facts.

~ TONI CADE BAMBARA

When the bonds that tie get knotted

Just as a litter of kittens can vary in color, hair length, and markings, so too can the emotional differences among siblings vary. Although each may come from the same environment and the same house rules, each has a unique path to enlightenment. Right action and right view is something only you can decide for yourself, not by or for others. Free your mind of tribal judgments, and dispel expectations. Own your personal truths, and allow for others to own theirs.

If you are patient in a moment of anger, you will escape a hundred days of sorrow.
~ CHINESE PROVERB

The truth about our childhood is stored up in our body, and although we can repress, we can never alter it.
~ ALICE MILLER

Put it in writing.
Write a note to individual family members telling them how they helped shaped your life in a positive way, or what you admire about them most and give specific examples. Mail it or leave it for a surprise discovery, on their pillow, in the coffee can, or bread box, preferably in a red, gold, rose, or green envelope.

Plant a different rose bush in your garden for each family member.
Roses traditionally mean love. When you tend to the needs of your rose bushes, you'll be reminded to tend to the needs of your family. Even if you and your family members are separated by disagreement, the rose bush (symbolized by its beautiful flowers and thorns that sometimes draw blood) is a wonderful way to connect with your roots and foster a loving heart. No need to allow the thorns to detract from the beauty of the blossoms.

One violet is as sweet as an acre of them.
~ MARY WEBB

FRIENDSHIP

Accept everyone.
It's easy to love those who love you back, but to accept and love those whom you do not know or those who do not like you is to accept everyone for who they are. All is one—this is Zen. Choose to be a friend to everyone.

A fool finds no pleasure in understanding, but delights in airing his own opinions.
~ UNKNOWN

Mail a rainbow.

Send a birthday card or a loving note to friends with whom you've lost touch. To know that you were thinking of them will light their hearts.

You can't clap with one hand.
~ CHINESE PROVERB

Extend your love both near and far.

Write a short note to friends near and far telling them how they've touched your life, provided you with comfort, or loved you unconditionally. The unexpected gift without attachment is a gift of love.

Heal a wound.

Reconnect with a friend with whom you've had a disagreement and allowed time to pass. Put difficulties in the past, and focus on the ways in which you've grown from the experience. A friend lost is but a flower left without water.

When a leopard dies, he leaves his skin; a man, his reputation.
~ CHINESE PROVERB

Savor the flavor of the moment.

Invite a friend to dinner, and indulge your favorite foods together, preferable those you eat with your fingers. Don't worry about calories or your weight. Be children delighting in the simple pleasures of sharing together.

Listen to all, plucking a feather from every passing goose, but follow no one absolutely.
~ CHINESE PROVERB

Learn to listen.

Only a fool listens and then concludes. Practice the art of listening, fully present without judgments or conclusions—alert, silent, open, and receptive. Accept what is being said.

Offer your services.

Ask how you can be of service to a friend, not why your services are needed. A friend will offer service gladly and openly, without expectations or the need for justification. Be a friend.

When you're thirsty, it's too late to think about digging a well.
~ JAPANESE PROVERB

Always be honest.

Being supportive isn't an excuse for lying to a friend. Be honest with your friends at all times so they'll rely on your love to soften a reality they already suspect.

Never take advantage of friends willing to give.

They may be out of gifts when your need is the greatest. We often turn to those who we know will care for our needs readily, those who find their value or self-esteem in assisting others. Taking advantage of their nature and insecurities is cruel. Ask for what you truly need and no more.

Respect the person first and the friendship second.

Being your friend shouldn't require others to compromise themselves or the needs of their family. Always respect other's differences of opinion and their responsibility to family time. Your time together shouldn't impose hardship or choice.

Thus nature has no love for solitude, and always leans, as it were, on some support; and the sweetest support is found in the most intimate friendship.

~ CICERO

Let opinions pass.

If you aren't asked your opinion, feel free to pass on giving it. With friends and family, we often take liberties with our opinions, standing on the closeness of our relationship as grounds for doing so. Find a way to be supportive without being judgmental or imposing your truths and expectations.

Allow your friends to grow and change.

A true friendship is one in which we're allowed to be ourselves. Just as we grow and change, so too must our friends—and we must accept these changes as they come. Such acceptance is not only love but Zen as well.

Be global.

Having a diverse group of friends can expand your world and your experiences. Find innocent wonder in different cultures, and you'll experience more of the world. Try different foods, attend cultural gatherings, and be open to different traditions.

Know when to say goodbye.

Friendships begin on what we view as a positive reflection of ourselves. Over time, that view may change as another's true nature puts us in conflict with our own beliefs. Don't blame, judge, or shame others. Know that you've experienced something that has forced you back to your own truths, and walk away, grateful for the experience.

Move beyond words.

Sometimes the sweetest moments with a friend involve no spoken words, and yet the conversation is endearing. Engage in hikes, needlepoint, music, and meditation with a friend.

Know that friendship comes in many forms.

The love you bring to a friendship may not be returned in the same form or intensity. The key is to remain loving in your own heart and grateful for the experience of it.

Smile.

Admission to the friendship party requires only a smile. Surround yourself with friends who make you laugh at nothing, easing the way of more complicated choices.

Seize the moment.

Friends point the way to sunlight during moments of darkness. Seizing the opportunity to help a friend in such a way opens both of your hearts. When friends are down, pick them up with your willingness to be there for them, acknowledging their pain.

WORK

Your work is to discover your world and then with all your heart give yourself to it.

~ THE BUDDHA

Create value in your everyday tasks.

Daily meditation expands your ability to concentrate deeply and remain mindfully focused with greater ease. Use this focus to do the best job that you can and to be the best you can be in your present work, without expectations of grabbing the golden ring at the top of the ladder.

Only when all contribute their firewood can they build up a strong fire.

~ CHINESE PROVERB

Whatever you can do or dream you can, begin it. Boldness has genius, power, and magic in it. Begin it now.

~ GOETHE

Experience your own vision.

Do what you love or long to do. Clear your mind of enemy tapes (It isn't a real job, or What about the family business? or You can't make any money doing that!) by sitting quietly and letting go of expectations or criticisms—yours and those of friends and family. Allow your mind to wander with a childlike "what if?" and feel the excitement without asking "how?" A still mind will intuit the avenues and answers you seek.

It is hard to fight an enemy who has outposts in your head.
~ SALLY KEMPTON

Bring meaning to your work area.
Keep a treasure vase in your work area symbolizing long life, wealth, and prosperity.

You must do the thing you think you cannot do.
~ ELEANOR ROOSEVELT

Create your dreams through visualization.
Cut out pictures from magazines that depict the work you'd like to be doing, cut out words and statements that support the feelings you

associate with such work, those that resonate within you. Make a collage that you can view daily, or put the cuttings into a large purple envelope (the color of prosperity), and explore them before each meditation. Visualize yourself already deeply involved with this work, and feel the balance in your life—that of fulfillment in your work and a sense of purpose.

If you hear a voice within you say "you cannot paint,"
then by all means paint and that voice will be silenced.
~ VINCENT VAN GOGH

Be a leader.
Be a leader not by position but by doing what needs to be done when it needs to be done—and for no other reason. This is Zen duty. Don't pass to another what you're capable of doing yourself. A leader asks no more from his subordinates that what he himself is willing to give.

Your vision will become clear only when you look into your heart.
Who looks outside, dreams. Who looks inside, awakens.
~ CARL JUNG

Value integrity, not position.
Position and money have no value without integrity. Believe in what you do at this moment, knowing that it will impact what comes next. Every action creates another action that affects both yourself and those around you. Make every action count for a positive outcome for all.

He begins to die that quits his desires.
~ UNKNOWN

Learn from your mistakes.
Success depends on how open you are to examining your failures. By accepting them, you learn the difference between surviving and being successful. Only then are you closer to your goal. It's impossi-

ble to succeed without failing first.

Take the first step in faith. You don't have to see the whole staircase, just take the first step.

~ DR. MARTIN LUTHER KING, JR.

Shine your own star.

It isn't enough to simply follow in the footsteps of one who has gone before you and paved the way. Leave your own path and landmarks of greatness for others to follow. Everyday, athletes break records in speed, height, catches, and home runs. How did they do it? They improved on what came before them, through training, endurance, strength, creativity, and healthy lifestyles.

Rest is not idleness, and to lie sometimes on the grass under the trees on a summer's day, listening to the murmur of water, or watching the clouds float across the sky, is by no means a waste of time.

~ SIR JOHN LUBBOCK

He who rides the tiger finds it difficult to dismount.

~ CHINESE PROVERB

Don't become a workaholic.

Like addicts who turns to substance abuse or alcohol as a means of numbing their pain, people often use work to mask their unhappiness or insecurities. Be mindful as you begin meditation. Ask yourself, "If I conquered the top of my professional world today, would I be happy?" Also, take note of the items that pass through your thoughts: family, friends, the abundant (or lacking) peace, places that come to mind such as your hometown calling you back. What will you have gained, and what might you lose? Allow these thoughts to float into your mind and disappear. Write down the images you felt more strongly and intuit their message.

The need for change bulldozed a road down the center of my mind.

~ MAYA ANGELOU

Cultivate right action into your work environment.

Cause no pain, do no harm, and be aware of suffering. Commit to protecting the lives of all people, animals, plants, and minerals. Be mindful of the suffering that oppression, stealing, and social injustice cause.

In the bigger scheme of things, the universe is not asking us to do something, the universe is asking us to be something. And that's a whole different thing.

~ LUCILLE CLIFTON

Act when your heart implores you.

You may never get a second chance. A moment lost to hesitation is a moment lost forever. When an occasion arises that lends itself to inspiration, honesty, or right action, don't miss the opportunity. Express who you are at all times. If you have an idea or opinion to contribute at a company meeting, voice it. Don't wait until afterward and shuffle it among coworkers.

Perfectionism is the voice of the oppressor; the enemy of the people. It will keep you insane your whole life.

~ ANNIE LAMOTT

Dress your desk.

Dress your desk with those things that inspire you, items that represent success and achievement—a photo, a special pen, a golden weight. Light the fire of creative energy with a handsome desk lamp. Fire (symbolized by the light of a lamp) is a Feng Shui cure for activating good chi (energy).

You must once and for all give up being worried about successes and failures. Don't let that concern you. It's your duty to go on working steadily day by day.

~ ANTON CHEKHOV

Take 5.

Begin each morning at your desk with 5 minutes of stillness, and write down the words or images that come to mind. You may find that certain things in your day correlate to these words or objects. Intuit, and you shall find.

The best thing that can come with success is the knowledge that it is nothing to long for.

~ LIV ULLMANN

Enjoy victory.

Place a victory banner at your workstation, symbolizing victory of activity (body, mind, and speech) over obstacles and negativity.

Poor by condition, rich by ambition.

~ CHINESE PROVERB

Never doubt that a small group of thoughtful citizens can change the world. Indeed, it is the only thing that ever has.

~ MARGARET MEAD

Be yourself.

Identify your work by how it touches others, how it assists in their lives, and why you're uniquely qualified to do it, not by the company name on your employee badge. How does your personal effort contribute to the lives of others? Meditate on the ways in which your true nature is present at work. If you present a different persona at work, ask yourself why. Is it really necessary to do so, or is it ego?

You must work, we must all work, to make the world worthy of its children.

~ PABLO CASALS

FORGIVENESS

Forgive yourself and others—and let go of the negative feelings.
When you judge someone, you're the one who feels the pain, fear, anger, and resentment within yourself. Sit quietly before the mirror in your mind, and ask yourself under what circumstances you would forgive the person you see in the mirror's reflection.

Don't hold hostage your emotions for another out of anger.
Get in touch with the true nature of your hurt in quiet meditation, and release it. Run your fingers through the grass or the leaves of a tree, allowing your negative energy to be absorbed and cleansed.

Seek balance.
Negative emotions (such as fear, shame, anger, and hate) are the body's way of telling us that we're out of balance. Sit quietly, and contemplate your emotion. Identify the root of it (for example, abandonment, violation, or rejection), and sense what part of your body is in pain or discomfort. Mediate on the corresponding chakra

until it's spinning freely with the essence of soft loving light and the pain subsides.

Holding anger is like grasping a hot coal with the intent of throwing it at someone else; you are the one who gets burned.
~ BUDDHA

Let go of blame.
Letting go of blame requires that you take responsibility for how you're feeling and responding to the situation. Take note of your tight shoulders, the pit in your stomach, and the weakness in your legs as you begin to breathe in quiet meditation. Repeat the affirmation, "I'm responsible for creating my own happiness." Then let go of any blame, and breathe.

Whatever pours forth from the mind
Possesses the nature of the owner.
Are waves different from the water?
Their nature like that of space is one and the same.
~ BUDDHA

Visualize forgiveness.

To not forgive another is to not forgive ourselves. By experiencing pain we grow, and from all growth we better understand ourselves. Look at past resentment from the perspective of the other, and understand that they too have suffered pain. Visualize their aching heart, and send them golden rays of forgiveness.

Focus on the action, not the person.

Don't confuse the person who has wronged with the wrong action. Circumstances, anxiety, and stress can cause anyone to fall from honor. Rise up against injustice with right action (being mindful and nonviolent), but above all, do so with compassion for the person who committed the injustice.

Obtain closure by putting pen to paper.

If you feel betrayed, lied to, cheated on, or harmed, write a letter to the person who caused you the pain. Begin with, "If I could write you a letter..." and go on to tell that person how their actions made you feel. Then imagine getting the ideal response from that person. What would they say that would make you feel loved, valued, and respected? Allow the emotions from such a response to travel through your body with soft glowing light, easing your muscles and letting your defensive body fall. When your mind is still, discard the letter (burn it, bury it, or toss it in the trash) as a sign of completion and closure.

WELLNESS

Cultivate a reverence for life.

Be aware of the suffering that stems from destruction of life—all life. Connect with nature, whether through hikes at nearby lakes and streams or through the single blessing of a wild poppy seed that found shelter in your yard and blossomed to delight your surroundings.

If at first you don't Zen, try, try again.

It isn't easy to change a lifelong pattern of subconsciously taking in the world and leaving it to your dreams to filter. Conscious living takes examination and thought—the effort to look at what you say, think, and do and ask yourself "Why?" instead of operating on autopilot. When you treat yourself as a beginner, you're more open to the learning experience. Start with ten minutes, and have no goal but to remain still and feel what rises to the surface. If nothing comes, accept it (don't expect a payoff) and continue the next day. As you learn to relax and be still in thought (or the practice of "no thought"), your payoff will come in blissful waves of self-understanding and in conscious thoughts and actions that will surprise you.

A man whose heart is not content is like a snake which tries to swallow an elephant.

~ CHINESE PROVERB

Nourish joy in yourself and others at all times.

Find humor and the hidden rainbow in daily events and marvel at the smallest of detail. Become alert to all that is alive around you. If a television commercial makes you cry, be joyful in the emotion. Feel, feel, feel! Don't think—feel!

Find the corner puzzle piece.

When you're suffering, find the conditions for happiness, and meditate on how to achieve them. Perhaps in stillness you'll find that they already exist. Realize that joy and suffering are intertwined and impermanent. Turning on joy can be as simple as turning on a light in a darkened room. Find the switch inside yourself.

Get a feeling for your feelings.

Learn to identify the difference between your "feelings" and your "self." Although we aren't purely made up of emotions, without mindfulness, we react to them. When a strong feeling appears, learn to embrace it and understand it; see it for what it truly is through meditation. With practice, we can control even the strongest urge to act upon an emotion, and instead seek the truth behind an event or circumstance.

"Weed" your mind.

Negative thoughts, perceptions, and judgments reside in the deep spaces of our consciousness. When a painful experience (or a perception of one) occurs, these negative formations are triggered automatically without awareness. Sit still and be aware of your body, specifically the part of your body in which you feel the perception. As you explore the mental formation of that perception and search for its origin, feel the changes that take place in your body. With practice, you'll learn to quickly recognize these mind-body reactions and, with mindful control, weed them out. Most important, you'll learn a more compassionate way to deal with the "seeds" of your emotions.

Make use of the fabulous five.

Five powers that help us generate energy within ourselves are faith, energy, mindfulness, concentration, and insight. Used together, faith promotes diligence (energy), which fosters mindfulness, which heightens confidence and results in insight (wisdom). Cultivate these seeds in meditation, and your harvest will be a joyful life.

Block out the chatter.

When your mind is full of endless chatter, stressed and consumed by deadlines, close your eyes and visualize the chatter as that of a television in your head, the messages running on like endless commercials. Now visualize clicking the OFF button on the remote. A black screen appears, and the sound and pictures disappear. Stay in the quiet of the darkened screen, and remain there until you feel calm and clear minded.

Alleviate stress and fatigue by practicing mindful body scanning.

Lie down with your eyes closed, and become mindful of your forehead while breathing. Use this energy to light your brain, your eyes, your ears, and your nose. Become more aware with every breath, and continue down to your heart, lungs, and stomach, loving each part. Smile to each part of the body with compassion and concern. Continue down, all the way to your toes. Your body will experience great relaxation and rest.

Return to stillness.

Attitude is key in zazen. After all, it's impossible to stop thinking entirely or to squelch the thoughts of others, bills, errands and such, at least initially. Recognize them, and let them pass. By doing so and returning to stillness, unconscious thoughts will begin to rise like bubbles to the surface on the ocean, because the mind will express. Acknowledge these thoughts, but don't follow them.

It is health that is real wealth, not pieces of gold and silver.

~ MOHANDAS GANDHI

Let go of the illusions.

Although desires are natural, they shouldn't be categorized as good or bad. Instead they should be viewed as bonno (which in Japanese means "illusion," "that which troubles the mind," or "false view") when associated with the attachments that we cling to or resist. Enlightenment is the complete letting go of all such illusions and freeing the mind to see and experience what "is."

I have lived on the lip of insanity, wanting to know reason,
Knocking on a door. It opens.
I've been knocking from the inside!

~ RUMI

Keep a gratitude journal.

Let go of expectations through gratitude. Expectations usually cause us to feel denied of some "thing," some payoff, or some experience. The true charms of life can be found only when you're open to events without expectation and grateful for their occurrence. By keeping a gratitude journal, you can acknowledge the many blessings you receive and increase them in your life a thousand times over.

Meditation is not the means to an end. It is both the means and the end.
~ KRISHNAMURTI

Experience new wu-wie.
From the quiet, nonjudgmental state of meditation, we can experience our true nature—a new way to be. From this newer, truer sense of being, new action that is neither premeditated nor disconnected will follow. New wu-wie (which in Chinese means "action that isn't forced") will resonate in grace and flow with the dance of life.

Trouble brings experience and experience brings wisdom.
– UNKNOWN

Strive to be calm.

It's possible to be actively calm even during times of chaos. Practicing to be both calmly active and actively calm at all times with a focused mind can increase your energy and enable you to complete your tasks more quickly. Through walking or sitting meditation, you train your mind to focus on everything, though nothing "in the moment," with clarity and calmness.

Only with cutting is jade shaped to use; only with adversity does man achieve the way.

~ CHINESE PROVERB

Embrace sorrow.

Sorrow, like joy, brings growth and fulfillment when we embrace it's presence and learn more about ourselves from it. All that is sweet isn't all meaningful.

Blame yourself as you would blame others; excuse others as you would excuse yourself.

~ CHINESE PROVERB

Connect with reflection.

Stop being a "habit hunter," turning to what you normally do when you normally do it, and reflect instead on how and why you've come to where and how you are. Inquire as to what your commitments are and to whom, your direction (or lack of it), and your goals. Do you focus your daily intentions on these areas? If you feel confused or irritated, recognize such feelings as wisdom, wisdom that perhaps you aren't acting out of self-love or sound spirit. Become a seeker of your own path through the footprints you've made. Reflection brings growth through the understanding of one's self.

Don't climb a tree to look for fish.

~ CHINESE PROVERB

Become more childlike.

Meditation can be like giving birth to the child within, as you allow, without influence, the true nature of your being to rise to the surface. Being unimpeded by the philosophy, opinions, and laws of tribal society offers freedom to feel, think, and play within your own light. When behaving childlike, you allow yourself to defy that which you've always told yourself and been told by others. Be like the toddler who has experienced the power of muttering the word "No!" aloud for the first time, dazed with excitement. Allow your mind to be innocent of learned thought and expression, and bless the child within.

And forget not that the earth delights to feel your bare feet and the winds long to play with your hair.

~ KAHILIL GIBRAN

Appreciate the opportunity to be in-between.

The discomfort of being in-between two states (bardo)—happy or sad, excited or fearful, angry or loving, working or unemployed—is fundamentally the training ground for the Middle Way. It involves being in the present, the now, the "not knowing." Embrace the discomfort, because as you become more secure standing in-between the two states, you rest completely in the present and experience clarity. It's the "not needing to know" a specific outcome or resolution that paves the way to enlightenment.

Learn from life's trials.

Life isn't a trial, but trials are a part of life. When you search for direction, search within. Accept what happens as what is, and don't be concerned with what could have or should have been. Meditation will aid acceptance and the message of the experience.

One single grateful thought raised to heaven is the
most perfect prayer.
~ G.E. LESSING

HAPPINESS

Go for the gold.

Life is never constant—that is, it never stands still, and it's never without a challenge. Find the gold in any change: the lesson, the opportunity, and the balance. We often hear the words, "If this ____ hadn't happened, I would have never have found ____." Don't wait to find the silver lining in change. Know that it's there and the experience of the change is where your heart and mind need to focus, which is always on the present.

If I just when the spirit moves me, the spirit will ignore me.
~ CAROLYN FORCHE

Be patient with yourself.

There is no proper place or time to begin Zen—you begin simply when you're in the present, with no goal in sight, when you're ready to just be. It may be helpful initially to follow your breath—that is, to be mindful of it—not counting the breaths but letting them flow with your thoughts, in and out with ease. Learn to quiet the noise both inside and outside your head, and you'll reap great rewards.

There is no highroad to happiness or misfortune; every man brings them on himself.
~ CHINESE PROVERB

Practice, practice, practice.

"If you help me now, God, I'll...." We've heard it said, and we've said it ourselves, as if only in a crisis is such assistance necessary or available. Mind, body, and spiritual wellness must be cultivated day-by-day, hour-by-hour, minute-by-minute—consciously, in our actions, thoughts, and words.

Thousands of candles can be lighted from a single candle, and the life of the candle will not be shortened. Happiness never decreases by being shared.

~ BUDDHA

Experience what you've touched.

Watch the light, your light, pass into another, and feel the joy you've shared from an act of kindness that brought happiness to another. Your own sense of happiness will grow tenfold with each experience. Savor the feeling and return to it often. Through it you'll give the gift of love to yourself.

Yellow gold has its price; learning is priceless.

~ CHINESE PROVERB

Start off your day on the right foot.

Begin your morning commute to work with an open and receptive heart. See the person in the car in front of you, not the car, and send that person your best wishes for the day. Feel your heart expand with golden, radiating light, and send it out to the landscape before you, touching all it comes into contact with. What you give will be returned throughout the day.

Life is a promise, fulfill it.
Life is beauty, admire it.
Life is bliss, taste it.
Life is a dream, realize it.
Life is a duty, complete it.
Life is a game, play it.
Life is sorrow, overcome it.
Life is a song, sing it.
Life is a tragedy, confront it.
Life is an adventure, dare it.
Life is luck, make it.
Life is too precious, do not destroy it.
Life is life, fight for it.
~ BUDDHA

Be open to what simply is.

Let go of longings for the past or the discomfort in an uncertain future. Practice zazen to maintain openness to the here and now, mindfully calm within the presence of "nothingness" without expectation. When you're open to all, all will come. If you lose your keys, tearing up the house won't help you find them. Instead, standing quiet for a moment and allowing your memory to rest may suddenly provide the answer to their whereabouts. This is Zen.

Be happy. It's one way of being wise.
~ COLETTE

Know the effects of your thoughts and your actions.

It matters little if you toss a large rock or a pebble into a pond. Both will send ripples of effect across the water's smooth surface. Be aware of the ripples you create, both kind and harsh. Everything spoken, thought, or acted upon has an effect, and that effect will come back to you.

One joy scatters a hundred griefs.

~ CHINESE PROVERB

Live in the present.

The "future" is an illusion that will never come. Make each moment a choice for the present—an action, a thought, or a word that supports your "now" and the world around you. By recognizing what we're feeling—recognizing that we can feel deeply, love deeply, and feel joy—we can demand that all parts of our lives produce that kind of joy.

Trying to understand one's self while still chained to hopes and fears prolongs the bondage.

~ BUDDHA

Seek absolute trust in your stillness, and truth will come.

Focusing on good and bad and gains and losses is a disease of the mind. With absolute trust, all striving disappears. If you're unsure how to approach a specific situation, mediate quietly to discern your true reason for the action and the way to best handle it. Trust that you know the right action.

Meditation brings wisdom; lack of meditation leaves ignorance. Know well what leads you forward and what holds you back, and choose the path that leads to wisdom.

~ BUDDHA

Know that the path leads on, not away.

Just before Ninakawa passed away, the Zen master Ikkyu visited him. "Shall I lead you on?" Ikkyu asked. Ninakawa replied, "I came here alone, and I go alone. What help could you be to me?" Ikkyu answered, "If you think you really come and go, that is your delusion. Let me show you the path on which there is no coming and going." With his words, Ikkyu had revealed the path so clearly that Ninakawa smiled and passed away.

Choose to lose.

Don't engage situations, individuals, or duties for the sake of being included, recognized, or accepted. If there is no value in your heart, there will be no value in your action. Choose to lose a job or identity that doesn't support your true fire.

Riches adorn the dwelling; virtue adorns the person.
~ CHINESE PROVERB

If there is light in the soul, there will be beauty in the person.
If there is beauty in the person, there will be harmony in the house.
If there is harmony in the house, there will be order in the nation. If
there is order in the nation, there will be peace in the world.
~ CHINESE PROVERB

Take a moment to reflect, as you wake up and before you go to sleep.

Upon waking up

Waking up this morning I vow with all beings,

To realize everything without exception, embracing the ten directions.

Before sleep

Going to sleep tonight I vow with all beings,

To calm all things, allowing the mind to be clear and pure.

~ CLOUDS IN WATER ZEN CENTER

See the interconnectedness of it all.

You don't need to practice Buddhism to find enlightenment in Zen. Meditation is deeply personal, as is the means by which you can understand your true nature and your connection to all things, regardless of your religion. Just as you wouldn't view waves as separate from the ocean's water, you aren't separate from another.

The passage is through, not over, not by, not around, but through.
~ CHERRI MORAGA

There are only two ways to live your life. One is as though nothing is a miracle. The other is as if everything is.
~ MOTHER TERESA

Appreciate the lessons that failure has to offer.
If you want to succeed fast, you must fail fast, for only through failing will you learn, grow, and experience your true goals.

We are what we think. All that we are arises with our thoughts. With our thoughts, we make our world.
~ BUDDHA

Commit to self-cultivation, and discover what makes your inner garden grow.

Tend to your garden's soil, and fertilize it with passion, tenderness, and faith. There's no such thing as a weed in the garden within: Everything has a purpose.

The worst loneliness is not to be comfortable with yourself.

~ MARK TWAIN

Talk to the universe through meditation.

When you meditate on your goals, you place your intentions within the universe, and it answers with auspicious signs, all of which provide a path to follow.

Courage is the power to let go of the familiar.

~ RAYMOND LINDQUIST

Accept and grow within the real deal.

Becoming the person you want to be isn't the same as becoming your true self. Life is a journey of change and your response to it. Strive to be your true self, not the illusion of who you want and wish to be.

Use your imagination not to scare yourself to death but to inspire yourself to life.

~ ADELE BROOKMAN (PSYCHOTHERAPIST)

Take one more step.

When you think you've gone as far as you can, remove from your mind the physical or emotional block. Visualize a clear path, and listen to the message that rises from within. The next step you take will renew your confidence and heart.

Anything that is of value in life only multiplies when it is given.

~ DEEPAK CHOPRA

LOVING-KINDNESS

Be friendly.

An act of loving-kindness means with complete and unrestrained friendliness. When the mind is at ease, it's friendly. A mind at ease evokes compassion and fearless wonder and is receptive to all, despite the circumstances. Children, until they're taught differently, are friendly. Returning to the child within through quiet meditation invites the child to walk with you in all that you do.

Wherever there is a human being, there is an opportunity for kindness.

~ SENECA

Make visible the invisible.

Everyday in the workplace, we pass those whom we may not know or collaborate with on a daily basis, failing to acknowledge their presence and contributions. Consciously seek to see them as a part of yourself, as part of the whole, and pass on a kind hello.

Count but only one reason.

Give what you can, because you can and for no other reason.

Open your caring heart, and imagine the Buddha-mind as light in your heart.

You need not know the one who suffers; perhaps he or she holds steady on a street corner, begging for change or food. Instead of looking away, draw on your compassionate Buddha-mind to ease their pain. Breathe in the suffering as darkness, and breathe out loving-kindness as healing white light. Allow the light to pass from you to the one who suffers and to illuminate his or her being. While transforming your own heart-mind, you'll help open a healing space for another.

Kindness is the language which the deaf can hear and the blind can see.
~ MARK TWAIN

Practice the art of collaborative giving.
Give back to the community and others around you by volunteering to work on a Habitat for Humanity house.

Help the homeless.
Offer to pick up any unsold clothing or bedding from a nearby estate or yard sale and distribute the items to a local shelter for the homeless.

If my hands are fully occupied in holding on to something, I can neither give nor receive.
~ DOROTHEE SÖLE

Engage your children and their friends in an "All Hands Club."

Set aside one day each month for the club, as a whole, to support others in the neighborhood. Encourage them to actively pursue neighbors close by (for example, elderly, sick, or disabled neighbors) who could benefit from a single day of yard cleanup, fence painting, or window washing. Even a half-day event each month would bring joy to others and fill the hearts of the children involved. Have other moms and dads contribute something to lunch afterward!

Joy is strength—Joy is love—Joy is a net of love by which you can catch souls.
~ MOTHER TERESA

Reach out to those who are less fortunate.

For those who are confined to their home or "shut in," life is a constant of going without, especially if they don't have others to rely upon. To help out, organize a biweekly grocery run with your children (and their friends) whereby each child (or pairs of children) fills a basket with items requested by someone who is unable to shop for himself or herself because of age, illness, or disability. You supervise and drive, and they deliver.

Dogs show no aversion to poor families.
~ CHINESE PROVERB

Teach your children through your actions.
Children are constantly hearing the phrases "Be kind," "Help your neighbor," "Don't hate," and "God loves everyone" at home, in school, and at church. Still, it's through your actions, not your words, that they take these notions to heart as truths. Right speech is nothing without right action.

There is only one real deprivation, I decided this morning, and that is not to be able to give one's gifts to those one loves most.
~ MAY SARTON

Conserve, conserve, conserve.
Conservation is an act of loving-kindness to the Earth—to all life and all beings, both plant and animal. Right action includes doing no harm to the environment. So remember to recycle product containers (glass, plastic, paper, and cans), conserve water with low-flow attachments and timing devices, and preserve groundwater supplies by properly disposing of poisons (oil, paint, and pesticides).

To talk good, that is not being good; to do good, that is being good.
~ CHINESE PROVERB

Mala (or Power) Bracelets

In Sanskrit, mala means, "string of beads." It's believed that the power of the mala bracelet stems from the uniqueness of the individual stones (or beads), each signifying a specific power. They can be used in meditation or worn throughout the day to enhance your intentions.

Turquoise—good health; brings good fortune; an antidote to poison

Amethyst—intelligence, thought to aid sobriety

Tigereye—creativity

Mother of pearl—wealth

Rose quartz—love

Aventurine—success, ease of mind

Wood—harmony (boxwood = longevity; birch = medicinal, the

   "spirit tree"; rosewood = considered auspicious)

Hermatite—antidepressant, healing of wounds

Quartz crystal—strength, purity

The Zen Way

Be childlike, experiencing life anew with wonder and enthusiasm. Be a beginner who's aware of nothing and everything, open and receptive. Listen, learn, and love.

Courage

Have the courage to stand true in your beliefs, despite the world at large. Have the courage to let go of truths you once believed that no longer serve you. Have the courage to become the real you when by yourself or among others.

Prosperity

A rich man is known not for what he has attained but for what he gives away. In Zen, when you become empty of wants and possessions, you make room for something greater. It's better to evaluate what you've grown to become, than what you've acquired.

Problem Solving

A dark room is easy to navigate once you turn on a light. A problem can be resolved as well by changing your perspective and concentrating on the solution instead of the problem. A closed mind sees only darkness. Always take your darkness (be it confusion, anger, or fear) inside yourself with meditation. Be still until you've understood your emotions and cleared them from your body by breathing and replacing darkness with light through visualization.

Truth

Truth can't be rationalized or made to confirm. What is, is nothing more, nothing less. Truth is something you feel and know without clarification. Our actions or words on truth's behalf are something that we manipulate without conscious effort and understanding. This is Karma. If you have doubts about truth, meditation will clear your head and reveal the truth to you.

The Present

The breath you're breathing in, the touch of your tongue to your lips. This is the present. Not yesterday's moment or tomorrow's desires. Live in the present with mindfulness and action. Make the most of every moment.

Contentment

Acknowledge the blessings that life brings to you. Have faith that the lessons and the gifts are for your greatest benefit. Don't segregate the good and the bad, because it all comes to you for a reason. Even the negative can and should be seen as a blessing—as an opportunity to grow and become stronger.

Compassion

Open your heart to others and know that they're doing the best they can. Your lessons aren't theirs, and judgment isn't yours to give. Understand the pain, sorrow, and struggles of others, and bless them with your love.

Joy

Joy flows from a river within you, not to be obtained through sheer desire, or achieved by outer goals. Let the river of joy flow unobstructed, unaffected by circumstance and others. When you smile at a butterfly taking from the sweet blossoms in your yard, feel joy, and be joy! Savor the emotion, and return to it often.

Loyalty

Be loyal to your own truths, your own heart in all circumstances. Be your own loyal subject, and you'll never walk alone. Make a list of those truths, the truths you would lay down your life for. Now live those truths.

The Journey

There is no beginning and no end, only the journey. Cherish each moment and let wisdom be your guide. It has been said that we need to toss out our plans in order to make way for our true purpose. Whether you search for your destiny or not, destiny will find you.

Be open to opportunities that offer growth, even if that path leads you in an entirely different direction.

Understanding

With each experience, loving or cruel, we grow. Accept each experience as an opportunity to discover more of yourself and your true being. This is Zen. For every downside, there's an upside, a chance to learn and respond with love. Meditation is all about learning to understand yourself so that in turn you may better understand others.

Clarity

Reflect all that you are in clear action and words. Live your truths in clarity. Spend a day in clarity meditation. Count to ten before you speak, in every interaction with everyone you meet for twenty-four hours. In those ten seconds, ensure that what you are about to say is clear, both to you and to whom you're speaking.

Suffering

Suffering follows wants and desires. Search for them, and you'll find only pain. Release them and contentment will arrive at your doorstep. What we think we need or want we strive endlessly for, creating havoc in our lives and hearts. Letting go of them allows you to release the pain that comes with attachment and be grateful for what you have. Cherish that which you have, and abundance will come to you.

Tranquillity

Tranquillity is a state of harmony with all, knowing that everything is as it's meant to be. Expecting nothing more from life than what you have today doesn't mean banishing your dreams. It means simply finding peace with where you are now and knowing that if tomorrow never comes, you're blessed in today.

Stillness

In stillness there is all knowing without excuse, conformity, or clarification. This is what meditation is all about. Spend twenty minutes a day simply being still, alone in a quiet room, quieting your mind.

Sincerity

When your actions are pure of heart, sincerity is in the lead. To act outside of sincerity is to have a motive, a need, or an expectation—greed. Sincerity can't be forced, because it comes freely from the heart.

Self-Acceptance

People must be able to accept themselves in order to accept the world around them. As neither good nor bad, your true nature is all that you are and all that you need be. Value yourself by your standards alone. If you fail at something, learn and take responsibility. If you succeed at something, praise yourself for having the courage and diligence to try. Above all, be the lord of your own temple.

This heart becomes one's meditation room.

~ ZEN SAYING

About the Authors

Colleen Sell, editor of the best-selling book series *A Cup of Comfort* and former editor-in-chief of the award-winning *Biblio* magazine, spins tales both tall and true from a forested hideaway in the Pacific Northwest.

Rosemary Roberts is a newspaper columnist, a magazine feature writer, and a contributing author in the anthology *Miracle of Sons*. Specializing in health care, she freelances from her home in northern California, where she's known for her work on issues of domestic violence, aging, mental health, and teen medicine. She continues her study of metaphysics, alternative wellness, and spiritual philosophies, including those from her ancestry of Gaelic origins. Rosemary is the adoring mother of one son, Sean.

Other books by this author: *10-Minute Celtic Spirituality* (Fair Winds Press, Feb. 2003).